OUT OF THE BLUE

Book One of the
Barley Ford series

Nettie Anderson

HEDDON PUBLISHING

First edition published in 2021 by Heddon Publishing:

www.heddonpublishing.com

eBook published by L. Jordan
Copyright © Nettie Anderson 2021, all rights reserved.

No part of this book may be reproduced, adapted, stored in a retrieval system or transmitted by any means, electronic, photocopying, or otherwise without prior permission of the author.

ISBN 978-1-913166-55-7

Cover design by Catherine Clark
www.catherineclarkedesign.co.uk

This is a work of fiction. Names, characters, businesses, places, events and incidents are either the products of the author's imagination or used in a fictitious manner. Any resemblance to actual persons, living or dead, or actual events is purely coincidental.

No part of this book may be reproduced or transmitted in any form or by any means, electronic or mechanical, including photocopying, recording or by any information storage and retrieval system, without written permission from the author.

To:

My parents, and my awesome family, who continually inspire me.

My husband, for making me smile, and keeping the flow of tea going.

David Merriweather, an English teacher who really did inspire the written.

OUT OF THE BLUE

CHAPTER ONE

Listening to the host introduce her, Daisy yawned and rubbed her eyes, hoping she could stay awake long enough to deliver her presentation. Lack of sleep was beginning to take its toll: she'd lost count of the number of nights she'd spent padding around her apartment like an agitated cat. She slipped her fingers into the waistband of her skirt, realising it was significantly tighter after all the midnight snacking she had been doing.

Tugging at her purple waistcoat, Daisy then smoothed the front of her cotton skirt, having already pulled her wayward caramel curls through a velvet scrunchy. Her regular attire of jeans and baggy sweaters had been set aside when she had started dressing differently to shift into the persona of her alter ego, author Alex Dennison.

Daisy felt reassured that her best friend and personal assistant Sarah would be sitting on the front row of this gathering in the community hall. A moment's relief settled on her. Sarah helped quell the overzealous nerves snapping around her tired brain. Patient, sweet Sarah who put up with all her rants and complaints.

Releasing a long sigh, she reminded herself she was here to give an insight into the workings of a professional author. Yet that instantly reminded her how she was beginning to feel more and more exhausted by slipping between the two worlds. Suddenly she heard herself being introduced by Susan Draper, chair of the Women in Unity group she was here to talk to today.

She'd done her homework on this group. Originally a book group, it had morphed into a group of women who now met regularly and talked. To help support each other through whatever traumas they had suffered – violence, loss, broken relationships. Some members wrote about their feelings and thoughts as a kind of therapy.

Daisy inhaled silently, then slipped into the shadows, letting Alex become her. She walked into the hall, acknowledging their applause with a grateful smile. Their energy and enthusiasm resonated around. Daisy was surprised by how many people had come to listen to her talk. There must have been nearly forty people present. She never realised it was such a large group. The frequent clicks of a camera from the side unnerved her. Susan had mentioned that a reporter from a local paper may be present. Women in Unity relied heavily on donations, so all publicity was helpful to them. It wasn't that she minded the publicity, it was more that she hated being in view. Her quiet life of solitude suited her better.

She took her position at the front of the hall, sat down at the side of the table and took a sip of water before addressing her audience. Daisy had a trusted format for talks like these. Beginning with a brief biography, then talking about how she got into writing, encouraged by being a runner up in a competition when she was seventeen with the story about a prince and princess.

The audience listened intently as Daisy explained that, having written and published two books of her trilogy, 'The Rose Water Chronicles', she was now writing the final book. Daisy thought better of sharing with the audience that she seemed to have the dreaded writer's block. Struggling on a daily basis with flow and where the story was heading, she was fretful about how she would ever complete it.

Earlier that morning, she'd received an email from her editor, Greg, stating that he thought her current draft was weak. Daisy had suffered a meltdown, feeling a mixture of disappointment, fury and a sense of dread that her talents had deserted her.

Shaking away the distracting thoughts, Daisy brought herself back into the room.

'Can you tell us what happens in the end?' someone in the audience asked.

'Afraid not!' said Daisy emphatically.

'I can't give anything away, but I will say that writing this final book in the trilogy is a bit like saying goodbye to an old friend – someone you have known for years but are parting from for all the right reasons. Doesn't mean you won't miss them.'

There was gentle ripple of laughter. Daisy scanned the sea of faces in front of her, noticing a woman sitting alone on the back row. A petite, dark-haired lady who seemed to smiling. As Daisy's eyes locked onto the butterfly clasp clipped on the emerald green scarf around the woman's neck, her heart lurched and her hand flew to her chest. A wisp of something danced at the edges of her memory. A trill of laughter caught on the wind. Fleetingly, she was a child again, high in the air of the tree swing her father had made in the garden.

'Alex, do you have any ideas for what you'll write next? Is there any chance you'll write about Ellodin again?'

A voice broke her reverie.

'Er, sorry, can you repeat that? I didn't quite catch it.'

'Sure, I was just wondering what you were going to write next. Will it be about Ellodin?'

Shuffling more upright, Daisy was starting to feel dizzy, even a little nauseous.

'I have a few ideas but honestly, I think I am in need of a holiday.'

Another ripple of laughter spread around the room and Daisy glanced to the back of the hall to see the woman smiling. There was something about her smile: it stirred recollection that remained just out of reach for Daisy.

She was beginning to wish this was over. Her eyes had started to become heavy and she was losing her concentration. She saw Susan stand up. Her shoulders immediately relaxed knowing it was nearly all over. All she really craved was to be able to close the door of her flat on the world and crawl back under her duvet.

'Thank you, Alex. It has been a real insight into your work. We very much appreciate your time. Now if that's it, can I thank you all for coming…'

A hand shot up in the air.

'Ah, Miriam, go on then, this has to be the last question for Alex,' Susan said.

'Alex, I hope you don't mind me asking, we all know your mum left when you were very young. I wondered how you coped with that. Mine left when I was six years old and my dad just turned to drink. Has your writing helped you cope?'

The taste of something unpleasant formed in her mouth. She paused for a moment to take a drink of water. There was always one personal question which wrongfooted her. After all this time she still wished she could handle them better.

'I don't usually talk about my personal life.' Daisy fidgeted, staring at the glass in her hand. The familiar tightness was locking itself around her. The tightening in her chest making it difficult for her to breath. The room began to swim before her as she attempted to stand up.

'Sorry it's just we all find that writing has helped us express our emotions,' Miriam said apologetically and sat down suddenly.

Daisy attempted a smile, 'I'm honoured to be invited and to share my love of writing. Yes, I suppose it has helped. It's just that...'

Steadying herself, she grabbed the edge of the table next to her. A sudden flash from the side startled her and she sank into the chair. A swirl of nausea rose in her throat as she gripped the sides of the chair.

Daisy was vaguely aware of Susan asking her if she was alright, then she heard Sarah's voice from somewhere in the blur around her.

'Daisy, what's happening? Are you okay?'

Daisy waved her hand at Sarah. 'I'll be fine, just give me a few minutes.'

Bending down, Sarah rubbed Daisy's back and stroked her hair from her face.

Very slowly, Daisy lifted her head, so relieved the thudding in her chest had quietened.

'I'm so sorry. I probably didn't have enough breakfast.' Daisy laughed weakly.

'What happened?' Sarah knelt down next to her.

Daisy shook her head. 'I don't know. I went dizzy. I'm so embarrassed.'

'Come on, if you feel okay let's get you back to the car.' Taking hold of Daisy's arm, Sarah helped her up.

As Daisy stood up, she realised she was surrounded by a circle of women. She could see something in their eyes akin to sympathy and understanding. There was a sense of camaraderie, even a protective sisterhood, which made her feel safe.

Miriam approached Daisy and put her arm around her.

'We've all been there Alex, please look after yourself and come back when you feel better.'

Nodding, Daisy felt the prickle of tears. She was nervous about Sarah cross-examining her, knowing it was inevitable that her best friend would insist on some explanation for what had just happened. It was time to face the music.

CHAPTER TWO

'Daisy, this place is a mess. Seriously, when did you last wash any dishes?' Sarah spoke as she came through to the living area with two steaming cups of hot chocolate.

Sarah cleared away a clump of clothes so she could sit down. Placing the cups on the coffee table, she turned to Daisy.

'Honestly Daisy, this place reminds me of my student house when I was at uni.'

Catching hold of her necklace, Daisy felt the familiar itch of tears forming. She didn't know how to explain it without it sounding like she was going crazy.

'Better now I'm home.'

'What happened back there?' Sarah pushed gently.

'I don't know, I went a bit dizzy.'

'Well, something is going on. Is it the book?' Sarah pushed.

Daisy groaned. 'Greg emailed me this morning. The draft is too weak. He's worried I've lost my thread. I was almost sick when I read it. Then I had this weird sensation. My heart was pounding so hard and I felt really woozy. It's eight weeks to the deadline and I don't think I can get there. Then there are the dreams...' It was useless to try and put Sarah off the scent.

'Dreams? What dreams?' asked Sarah, blowing the top of her chocolate.

'About Mum. When she was still at home. I thought I could just ignore them. I don't want to remember them because it hurts too much. Then, when that lady Miriam asked me about why I write, I don't know, I just dissolved. Like I just panicked but I don't know why,' Daisy's voice trembled.

'You mean it's happened before?' Sarah asked, frowning.

Daisy nodded.

'Why haven't you said anything? Have you seen a doctor?'

Daisy's head shot up.

'No, why would I?'

'How about because this is serious.'

Daisy fell back against the cushions. It was like being caught in a whirlpool and she was drowning.

'I don't get it. It's been years since your mum bailed on you and your dad.'

'I've no idea. Except, sometimes it feels like Daisy Tremaine has been sucked away and replaced by Alex Dennison. I've attended so many events lately, having to cram my writing in when I get home. I haven't looked at my blog in weeks. Now these flashbacks are crowding in on me. You're right, after all this time you would think it wouldn't bother me, I'm nearly thirty for goodness' sake.'

'Maybe I should call your dad? Have you talked to him about any of this?'

'No. He thinks I work too hard as it is. I don't want to worry him.' The last thing she needed was her dad fussing around her. 'I just need to catch up on my sleep. Maybe eat more.'

'He's your dad Daisy, he's meant to worry. How come you are not eating or sleeping? You're starting to worry me. It was scary to watch you. One minute you were the professional, confident Alex and then wham, you just disintegrated.'

Daisy sipped her hot chocolate, desperately wanting to retreat to her bed.

'I don't want to be an alarmist but I think you had a panic attack.'

'A panic attack?' Daisy almost choked.

'Yes. Just look around you, if your head is anything like this chaos then something isn't right. Don't freak out, but I think you need to talk to someone.'

Lifting her head, Daisy stared at her friend. Her heartbeat quickened.

'What do you mean? I'm talking to you.'

Taking hold of Daisy's hands, Sarah took a deep breath.

'I mean professionally, as in a therapist. Who knows, if you had spoken to one years ago about what happened, you might not feel like this now. You are at a point in your life where you need to be completely focused and you're not. Or possibly, you just need a break. Burnout happens, remember Mark Drewton we were at school with? He collapsed at work and is now in some retreat in deepest Ireland.'

The two friends faced one another. Daisy was a little shocked by her friend's words. Slowly, she pulled her hands away.

'A therapist? You think I'm mad?'

Daisy began picking at her fingers. She noticed her chewed nails. When had she first started biting her nails?

'Of course not. Panic attacks, anxiety issues... they are serious. Why do you think those women at the group support one another? I read they've all suffered some form of trauma or emotional distress. That's why they formed the support group. Perhaps talking to someone will help you control your anxiety.'

'Oh, I don't know Sarah, what if news got out? You make it sound really serious.'

'Yeah, well that's because it is serious.'

Daisy shrugged her shoulders and carried on drinking her chocolate. Having done her own research into Women in Unity, she could empathise with the sense of abandonment some of them felt.

'What if you take yourself off somewhere? Go to a retreat. A holiday cottage, anywhere. No distractions. Think about it.'

Standing up, Sarah checked her phone.

'It's getting late and it's probably best you get some rest. I'm off. Text me if you wobble and I'll be straight over.'

'I promise.' Daisy closed the door and walked back into the lounge.

Snuggling under a fleecy throw on her sofa, Daisy thought about Sarah's suggestion of therapy. She could not begin to imagine sitting in front of a stranger and spilling her darkest, deepest secrets. When she had started to wrestle with finding her flow, she assumed it was writer's block and that was the reason for her becoming so anxious. Daisy had never had a problem knowing what to write; on the contrary, it was often all she could do to stop writing. Her brain evolved a storyline at amazing speed, often leaving her drained. It was this frenetic energy that drove her wild sometimes. She lay back and closed her eyes, desperate to zone out from everything. Daisy slipped into a welcome sleep, a break from the melee that had become her life.

CHAPTER THREE

The buzzing surrounded Daisy as she was walking through a garden. An abundance of bees and butterflies were fluttering around her. The low-pitched drone grew in its urgency as she attempted to bat away the insects she felt flying around her head. Slowly opening her eyes, the echo of the sound still played in her brain. Slowly, lifting herself up from the sofa, she realised it was the buzz of her intercom.

Reluctantly, Daisy sat up and rubbed her eyes before stumbling to the door to answer it.

'Daisy, it's Dad. Can I come up?'

'Oh, hi Dad, yes sure.' Daisy let out a long sigh and pressed the button. Good old Sarah. She must have called him.

Once inside, Dan Tremaine enveloped his daughter in a big bear hug.

'Daisy, Daisy, what's going on? Sarah rang me, she's worried sick.'

Gently easing herself out of her dad's arms, Daisy shrugged her shoulders, wishing Sarah had left well alone. She had no wish to begin explaining to her dad about the dreams of her mum.

Dan dropped into the only armchair, glancing around her apartment as he did so.

'I don't think I've ever seen this place look so untidy. You look pale Daisy, want to share what's going on? Sarah tells me the local gazette are reporting online that you are suffering from exhaustion. Are you?'

Daisy hovered by her desk. Staring out of the window, she wondered how she had reached such a low point. *What was The Gazette doing reporting such assumptions? Where did they get that from? Is that how she had appeared?*

'Sarah seems to think so. I don't know. I think I just need to finish the book, then have a holiday and I'll be fine.'

'Why didn't you call me? You know I'm here for you.'

'I know you are, Dad. Until yesterday I thought I had it all under control. But clearly I didn't realise how tired I was.' Daisy braced herself for the questions he would ask.

'Is it the book? Are you stuck?' asked Dan.

Still feeling reluctant to say too much, she did her best to swat away his concerns.

'I'm dragging my heels on the final draft. It's just taking me a bit longer than I thought to finish the final few chapters. I'll get there.'

'I'm more than happy for you to run your ideas past me. In the beginning you were always asking my opinion.'

'I know. You were always a great listener. I suppose as the story has evolved, I've needed to do that less. Maybe I know the characters much better now and I'm more confident in where they are going.'

'Doesn't sound to me like you are confident. Any chance of stalling the deadline?'

A sickly feeling began to rise within her as Daisy fought to control herself. She could feel the familiar knot tighten inside her chest.

Dan went over and put his arm around her.

'I can't help you, Daisy button, if you don't talk to me.'

'You haven't called me that in a while.' A little sliver of warmth spread through her.

'You have been a bit edgy lately. Goodness, you're shivering, come and sit down.'

Daisy felt her lips tremble as he steered her towards the sofa. The last thing she needed was her dad being nice to her. It just made it worse. Yet it had been just the two of them for so long, how could she shut him out?

'The thing is I'm not sure how to explain it all.'

'I'm listening.' Dan wrapped the fleecy blanket round her shoulders.

'It's weird but I keep having these dreams about Mum. Flashes from when I was growing up. I can't seem to make sense of them. It's like they are fragments of memories... and then they're gone. After all this time it doesn't make any sense. Sarah thinks I need to talk to someone.'

She felt her dad's arm stiffen around her shoulder.

Daisy stared at him, noticing the deep frown lines and the hint of grey streaking through his hair. A lump lodged in her throat.

'Wow, I wasn't expecting that. It's so long ago. What were you, ten at the time? There was a prestigious awards ceremony the Monday night before she left. I'd been nominated for a major travel writing award. The days leading up to it had been intense. Your mum had been erratic and clearly pre-occupied. An hour before we were due to leave, we had a huge row. The following morning, I woke up alone.'

'Do you remember all those times I hovered by the window, waiting? I waited every night for her to walk through the door. Rushed home from school expecting her to be there. Convincing myself it would be the next day. One more sleep and she would be home. I used to ask you all the time, how many sleeps till she came home?'

'Relentlessly,' Dan said, half smiling.

Hugging the blanket around her, Daisy bounced her knees up and down. Suddenly questions hovered and she knew there were answers she had never had.

'I understand nothing is ever straightforward, Dad, but did you ever work out why she left? You've never really talked about it. Actually, we rarely talk about it. Nor why you never divorced her. I mean she was there one minute, gone the next.'

Pulling himself up from the sofa, Dan walked over to the window.

'It was complicated. Relationships are, you know that. I focused on you and work. I'm not sure dragging all this up now is helpful' He pushed his hands further into his trouser pockets.

Daisy noticed his shoulders straighten, but heard the rasp in his voice.

'If talking helps us perhaps it is time we talked. There are things that don't add up, that I have never understood and never spoken to you about. It's like you are shutting me out.' Daisy shivered slightly, knowing she was crossing a line.

'What else is there to say? Is there any point? These dreams are probably no more than your stress over the book. Get that finished and you'll be fine.'

Daisy noticed the stubble on her dad's chin. The lump grew in her throat. When had the grey started to creep into his lush brown hair? Faint lines had etched themselves around the corners of his eyes. She had never thought of him growing old, yet stealthily it was marching through him. There was a reluctance in his voice to say any more. As if he was hiding something.

A sensation of drowning washed over her and it dawned on her that she'd been drowning for months, unable to speak to anyone about the relentless torture ripping through her. How her long nights of frenetic typing held the nightmares at bay. Trying to hold it together at events and be the professional she was meant to be. Inside she was broken and couldn't find a way to mend herself. It was clear from the tone in her dad's voice that he wasn't going to be drawn into saying anything else. Who knows, maybe he was right, all she needed to do was focus on the finishing line.

'Sarah mentioned to me that if you could get away, have a change of scene, it might help with at least finishing the book. What do you think?'

'Sounds like you and Sarah have had quite a chat. But yes, she did suggest it.'

'There's a place I know of. Barley Ford. It's very rural, very remote. Not even a village, more a collection of dwellings. There's a pub, I remember that.'

Glancing around her flat, Daisy recalled how ecstatic she'd been when her dad had agreed help her to buy it. It had been a momentous step for them both, having lived for so long together, yet she had loved being here. Her own little sanctuary. These days it felt more like a prison. She couldn't recall the last time she had visited anywhere that hadn't been connected to promoting her work. She wasn't sure how she felt about going on her own, even though she spent most of her time on her own in an imaginary world. Still, if it helped her sort her scatty brain out then she should just go. If these panic attacks or whatever she was experiencing didn't fade then she could consider seeing a therapist. For now, her book had to be the priority.

Daisy rubbed her forehead with her finger tips.

'Do you really think it will help?'

Dan stepped closer.

'If it helps you get to the end of that blasted trilogy, then yes. Barley Ford is far enough away to feel you have shifted locations but near enough for Sarah and I to check in on you if you need us to. From what I remember it was used for restorative purposes during the war. Like a kind of spa in its day. Let me give my contact a call and see what I can sort out. Let me do this for you, Daisy.'

Daisy nodded, acknowledging she was beaten and needed the support.

CHAPTER FOUR

Within twenty four hours an apprehensive Daisy was on her way to Barley Ford. Her dad had not only managed to secure a cottage for six weeks, but had managed to persuade the lady who took the booking to add on an option to extend.

'On my own though, Sarah? It's ages since I've been away,' Daisy remonstrated. She was busy packing while on the phone to her friend.

'Listen to yourself, you go everywhere doing book signings. Nights in swanky hotels, rubbing shoulders with the hoi polloi. Anyway, I can visit. Don't forget to take some warm clothes and footwear that you can tramp around the countryside in.'

'Great, it's one glamourous thrill after another. By the way, the last time I stayed anywhere it was a very questionable B&B. I can see I have no way out. I'll call you when I get there.'

It was late into the afternoon when Daisy reached the hamlet of Barley Ford. Tightening her grip on the steering wheel, she cautiously drove over an old stone bridge which looked as if it would collapse at any minute. As she edged her Mini over the narrow structure, she could just make out tendrils of plants clinging to the craggy surfaces of the aging stones. Following the curve of the road it opened out from the narrow lane to what she assumed must be the centre of the village. Slowing almost to a stop to take in her surroundings, Daisy's breath caught in her throat. The village appeared out of a clutch of trees and she was immediately drawn to the weatherworn Celtic cross taking centre stage on the village green. To her right stood a timber framed building with swinging sign. Daisy could just make out the faded lettering. The Merchant Moon. *Strange name for a pub*, she thought. Clustered together, to her left were a row of stone cottages each with a small garden to the front.

A movement startled her as she glimpsed out of the passenger window. An elderly gentleman was bent over, watering his garden. As if aware of being watched, he stood up and turned around. Pressing the button to lower the window she called, 'Excuse me!'

Ambling through his gate to her car, the breeze ruffled his silver hair, which he pushed back from his face as if irritated by its lack of discipline.

'Sorry to bother you, I'm looking for Blueberry Cottage.' Daisy waited as the man lowered his head to reply to her.

'Afternoon Miss, further up this road you'll see a lane, curving away to the left, Weavers Lane End. There are three houses. Blueberry Cottage is the last one.' He grinned. 'It stands on its own. Here for a holiday?'

'More to work without being disturbed. Hopefully a bit of downtime too.'

'It's the reason why most people venture here. I live just here, in Hector's Cottage. I dare say Dorothy will be waiting for you.'

'Dorothy? Oh yes Miss Swift. Well thanks for your help. I'll leave you to your watering.'

'Goodness don't call her Miss Swift else you will be swiftly on your way.' A slight harumph followed. 'You are very welcome, my dear. I'm Gerald by the way, welcome to Barley Ford.'

With that, he sauntered back to his garden. Musing over his comment about Miss Swift, Daisy continued driving. Spotting the turn, she was grateful she was driving her Mini, small enough to negotiate yet another narrow lane.

Reaching the end of the row of houses, Daisy caught sight of the wooden sign on the gate. Blueberry Cottage. The front of the cottage appeared to be enveloped by a large number of small shrubs. Laughing as she parked the car, she deduced these could be blueberry bushes, although she didn't have a clue what a blueberry bush looked like. Daisy swung open her door, stretched her long legs out of the car and climbed out.

'Hello my dear, you must be Daisy.'

Daisy flinched with surprise as she saw a small lady hunched over, hurrying towards her. Dressed in a thick woollen hat, an oversized raincoat and bright red wellies, she was holding a basket and at the same time trying to control a small barking dog.

'Harry, that is enough. Goodness, my dear, I didn't mean to startle you. We were off on our walk and I thought I would drop this off now.' She held out the basket.

'I'm Dorothy, Dorothy Swift. I spoke to your father. I live behind that bright red door.'

Dorothy twisted herself to point back in the direction she had come.

'Hi Miss Sw... er, Dorothy. Great timing, I've literally just arrived.'

'Shall we?' Dorothy clicked the latch on the gate and it swung open. It opened onto to a stone path leading to a dark timber door under a canopy.

'Oh, thank you, is this your cottage?'

'Oh no my dear, I keep an eye on it for the owner. On your own?'

'For now. My friend Sarah may come over at the weekend.' Daisy surprised herself at how much she was looking forward to seeing Sarah. Clearly Miss Swift liked to know what was going on. Daisy hoped she wasn't one of these village busybodies.

Following Dorothy down the path, Daisy's eyes flitted everywhere, trying to take in her new surroundings. She noted the date above the door, 1765. With a slight shiver, Daisy hoped there were no ghosts. There were enough of her own floating around.

'Shall I take the basket for you? You look like you have your hands full.'

'Why don't you take Harry? He's all noise, no action. A real character. A little stiff on his legs but then I'm no spring chicken myself. There we go, that's got it. You have to jiggle the handle. In we go.'

The door finally gave way and as Daisy held the dog's lead, a sense of apprehension began to overwhelm her. The gloomy interior of the hallway caused her to shiver again. Dark wooden stairs to the right curved their way upwards. To the left, Daisy could just make out a small lounge. Her dad had explained there was no website for her to check out the cottage as it was all word of mouth. This had made Daisy a little uncertain of what to expect and what kind of place she was coming to. Although the entrance hall was quite dismal and a little neglected with faded décor, it did have a certain charm. Her apprehension gave way to a strange sensation of being gathered and held.

'It's charming. I didn't know what to expect. It's not on any website.'

Dorothy halted in the middle of the hall and turned to face Daisy.

'Website?' Dorothy made a derisory noise. 'Oh no, you won't find us on any website. All word of mouth. Much better that way.'

While Daisy tried to avoid tripping over a very enthusiastic Harry, she wondered why it was better not to have a website. Dorothy's brusque manner indicated to Daisy that she had done this many times, introducing visitors to the cottage. Through the dim corridor, she was astonished to see it open up into a brightly-decorated kitchen, with a small snug at the far end and a blazing log burner.

'Goodness, this is amazing. Those views. It's lovely, Miss Swift. Oh, and there's a window seat too. That's just the place for me to work. That sofa also looks very inviting.'

'Call me Dorothy. I've never been married and no intention of doing so. Now there's milk, eggs, cheese and some bacon in the fridge. I put them there this morning but in the basket is fresh bread, some fruit cake and other bits and bobs.' Dorothy busied herself putting things away.

'I hope you'll enjoy your stay here, Daisy. Barley Ford is a sleepy little place on first glance, but don't be deceived. It has a very real beating heart. If you need anything, come to the red door. Oh yes, and The Merchant Moon holds a quiz night every Friday, so if you do fancy company, pop in. You'll meet quite a few of the locals. An interesting bunch.'

'A strange name, The Merchant Moon,' Daisy commented.

'Many centuries ago, the Lord of the manor used the building for discreet nightly meetings. Always involved jugs of ale and raucous shenanigans. I'm sure the locals will regale you with the legends. You'll be made welcome. Do go.'

'Yes I will do, but initially I yearn a great deal of quiet.'

'Hmm. Your father did explain you had a work project to finish. You will certainly have quiet here. Anyway, I must be off.'

Dorothy relieved Daisy of Harry, who was still very excitable.

'I almost forgot. If you want to use either of the log burners the instructions are on the side. I lit this one this morning, there is still a nip in the air. Tom Weaver leaves a supply every week by the back door so don't be alarmed if there's a stranger in the garden. Well, I'll leave you to it.'

Seeing Dorothy to the front door, Daisy came into the porch and pointed to the date above the door.

'I noticed the date, It's very old.'

'Oh yes, many of these cottages have been here since the days it was a country estate. They all have tales to tell. When you are at a loose end, I'll be happy to share them with you. Come on Harry, let's find those rabbits.'

Daisy watched as Dorothy walked briskly down the path. From her diminutive stature it looked as if a gust of wind would carry her away. But Daisy had an inclination that there was more to her than met the eye. A slight breeze ruffled the bushes next to her and Daisy was aware of the crispness of the air. The breeze carried a fragrance of earthiness on it. Lifting her head higher, the breeze brushed across her skin and lifted her spirits. She hadn't known what to expect, but was brightened by her first impressions.

'First things first Daisy girl, unpack the car.'

With the car emptied, Daisy decided to leave her luggage at the bottom of the stairs. Desperate for a drink, she went into the kitchen and clicked the kettle on. Whilst waiting she gazed through the large picture window which looked over the garden at the back. There was an air of neglect even though the grass had been recently mowed. Even more puzzling was the gate in the fence at the bottom of the garden. In the field beyond, sheep peacefully nibbled away. Maybe there was a footpath she could explore when she settled in. She wasn't really a walker but perhaps it would help to still her mind if she had a wander. Nearer to the back door was a bird table and an occasional bird swooped down to gather whatever remained.

'Well birdies, I can see I will have to feed you as well.'

Finding her way around the kitchen, she discovered the fruit cake and buttered a piece, then layered it with cheese. Settling herself on the window seat in the snug, Daisy could hardly believe she was here. The heat from the burner lulled her into a state of sleepy relaxation. Pulling her phone out of her pocket, she texted her dad to let him know she had arrived.

Before having chance to call Sarah, her phone beeped.

'Are you there? What's it like?'

Laughing, Daisy sprayed fruit cake all down her jumper.

'Well, I'm eating home-made fruit cake and lounging on a window seat watching a large grey horse munch grass at the end of the garden'

'What, there's a horse in the garden?'

'No, idiot, it's in the field that backs onto the garden. There are sheep too. It's wonderful Sarah. I have to concede that you and Dad were right to push me to come here. Dorothy is a hoot. She's a bit like Miss Marple. A game old bird I bet.'

'Fabulous. I look forward to meeting her then. Keep me posted and sleep well before you start tomorrow. Bysie bye.'

Sarah clicked off before she had chance to respond to their familiar greeting which had started at school and carried on into adulthood. Inky clouds started to float across the sky, evening was approaching.

The initial elation of arriving eased away as she remembered why she was here. Resting her head against the cool glass, Daisy could not hide from her sense of being alone. Her dad had been her world when her mum had left. Together they had muddled through many difficulties, including the moody teenager years. Being on her own had never bothered her before and she couldn't help being puzzled as to why it bothered her now.

A knock on the kitchen door made her jump. She smiled as she realised it was the old lady she had met earlier.

'Dorothy, hi, please come in.'

Holding the door open, Harry scuttled in and Dorothy followed.

'I hope you don't mind me calling in again but I quite forgot to give you the keys to this door.' She handed Daisy a key.

'No problem. I've just been enjoying your delicious fruit cake. I haven't even unpacked yet. It's glorious and peaceful. I was just wondering about the gate at the bottom of the garden.'

'Ah yes, it leads to a couple of footpaths. Do you hike?'

'Not really, though my friend Sarah insisted I bring a pair of walking boots just in case. I'm glad I listened to her.'

'I'm pleased your initial impression is favourable. One or two of our residents have left the city for Barley Ford. It has a certain draw.'

Dorothy hesitated before continuing.

'I know this may seem a little presumptuous but I have a meat pie cooking and there's far too much for Harry and I. Would you like to join me? I quite understand if not. After all, we have only just met. But there you are, Daisy, strangers yet to be friends.' Dorothy had a short, sharp laugh and Daisy was quite touched by her offer.

'That is so true and very kind of you. You know, I would love to. I am rather tired and I'd only make toast and curl up in bed.'

'Right then how about sixish? Remember we are the red door. Come along Harry, let's go. See you later Daisy.'

With that Dorothy left, closing the door firmly behind her. Daisy began to ponder that maybe this place wouldn't be too bad after all.

CHAPTER FIVE

Stretching her arms above her, it took Daisy a few minutes to orientate herself to her new surroundings. Lying still, she was acutely aware of the silence peppered only by bird song. It was as if she had landed in another universe. Languishing under the covers of a bed large enough for Daisy to spread out in, she surveyed her new bedroom. Decorated in pale lemons and off-whites, it enhanced the brightness of the sun sneaking through the opening of the curtains. The room was sparse in terms of furniture, with just a built-in wardrobe and a chest of drawers, but it had a peaceful appeal.

Remembering the feast Dorothy had served up for dinner, Daisy still felt stuffed and was sure she wouldn't need breakfast. Surprisingly, it had been a very pleasant evening. Dorothy was interesting and a very chatty host. Daisy had loved the gossip about her various neighbours, particularly Maud who lived next door to Dorothy, behind the blue door. Daisy thought it was strange being identified by the colour of your door. One thing was for sure: Barley Ford may appear sleepy, but from Dorothy's anecdotes last night, it was anything but. The story about Rob and how he came to be the landlord of The Merchant Moon was something out of a book. He'd won the pub in a do-or-die poker match. Bet all his savings and everything he had on the throw of a dice. He won. Daisy grinned to herself. Could it really be true? Imagine coming away on holiday and ending up staying because you won a pub.

Dorothy's cottage was cosy and welcoming and Daisy had been taken aback by all the books lining the walls. Dorothy had explained she had been a researcher during her working life and had since turned to local history. Daisy had toyed with telling her about being an author but decided against it. People's reactions were varied when she told them. She'd save it for when the time was right. Apart from anything else, she was quickly realising that just being Daisy was something to be relished.

Throwing back the duvet, Daisy slid out of bed and went to open the curtains. Staring out over the garden she was able to see a line of trees to one side and to the other side, a sparse area with very little grass but divided into sections by wooden frames. It looked like it could once have been a vegetable patch. The greenhouse had very little glass left in it. Next to it stood a broken down shed and Daisy was instantly struck that at some point, this had been someone's home. What had happened to the occupants, she wondered, to leave such a beautiful place? Perhaps Dorothy would know. Daisy made a mental note to ask her.

Directly beyond the back fence, the field had an incline so you couldn't see beyond. The huge grey horse was still standing by the rickety gate. She smiled as his tail flicked away unwanted flies. Without warning, an unbidden memory floated down and lodged itself. Her mum would take her riding at weekends when she was home. Usually on a Saturday morning when her dad was tucked away in his study, busy writing or fielding calls. Her vision became blurry as tears began filling her eyes. The tug of the memory caused her to recall begging her parents for a horse, her mum eventually caved in and negotiated a compromise. If she enjoyed the trial riding lesson, they would consider regular lessons. Although Daisy had adored horses, at age nine she had not calculated their size and when she came in close proximity to one, it had terrified her. With the help of the riding instructor, they had coaxed her gently into meeting Arthur. The strategy paid off because Daisy fell in love with Arthur and went for lessons every week. She hadn't thought about that in years.

A loud neighing snatched away her recollections as Daisy watched the horse lift his head. The sound of crunching on the gravel below her window made her step back slightly. She caught a glimpse of a dark shadow. Then clattering and banging. Unperturbed, she pulled on her hoodie and yanked on her booty slippers as she rushed from the bedroom and down the stairs.

Unlocking the back door, she was met by a very tall man and the darkest eyes she had ever stared into.

'Morning, didn't mean to disturb you. Still in bed?' A soft lilting burr hummed as he spoke.

Daisy hastily tugged her hoodie down and realised she was wearing the flimsiest of pyjama bottoms.

'I was just getting up actually when I heard a noise. Who are you?' Daisy was determined not to be intimidated by any country yokel.

'Tom, Tom Weaver, your local log man, tree-feller, mole catcher, you name it. Dorothy assured me she'd mentioned I was calling in with logs. Still a bit nippy at night in these parts. Spring confuses us into thinking winter is done.'

Daisy, caught off guard by his familiar tone, felt a flush in her cheeks. She wondered if she should offer to pay him or was it polite to offer a drink?

'Well, you sound busy. Do I owe you for the logs, I'm not sure what the arrangement is? It's all been a bit last minute coming here. Do you want coffee?'

Gabbling away like an idiot she started to grin, realising she was blathering rubbish.

'Maybe we should start again, eh?' He held out his hand, which was the size of a dustbin lid. Accepting his handshake, her own hand disappeared. Although Tom's hand was rough and calloused, there was a warmth and strength to it that sent a sizzle of heat through her.

'Tom Weaver. My farm sits in the dip beyond the rise of the field. Those are my sheep you can see. The horse is called Bentley, he belongs to my sister.' He pointed to the uneven wooden fence framing the back of the garden.

'Daisy Tremaine, blathering babbler. Would you like tea, coffee? I'm just about to make some.'

Aware she was still holding his hand, Daisy felt caught off guard. Withdrawing her hand, she tucked it into her pocket as if she wanted to savour the intimacy of his touch. Shaking her head to rid the image, she stepped back further into her kitchen.

'Another time perhaps, I have a trailer full of logs to distribute. Nice to meet you, Daisy Babbler. Enjoy your stay.'

With that he turned and marched away but not before he turned to look back at her. With a broad smile and wave, he was gone.

Momentarily held by his broad smile, a warmth emanated from her hand still tucked into her pocket. Closing the door with some reluctance, Daisy was left with a strange sensation. Rubbing the back of her neck she heard a growl from her stomach. Breakfast was calling after all.

Making coffee and pouring cereal into a bowl, she wandered through to the living room at the front of the cottage. *Whoever had previously lived here had really liked window seats*, she thought, sitting herself down. Perhaps it was the pull of watching the world slowly drift by. Not that much did drift by. Yesterday, after unpacking the car, she had discovered a large wooden gate further along the lane with a sign heralding Weavers Farm. Ping! Ah yes, Tom Weaver of Weavers Farm. Must be quite someone having a lane named after you. He was a bit more than log man and mole catcher.

Sipping the remains of her coffee, Daisy quietly laughed. Wait till she told Sarah about farmer Tom. She could just imagine her comments. None would be very ladylike. He was rather delicious despite his shabby appearance and course hands. Relationships were a bit of a disappointment to Daisy. It had been over a year since she had dismissed the last man. He'd been a complete jerk. He was forever posting selfies on Instagram, stating he was her muse. Daisy soon became wise to his enjoyment of the limelight and sent him on his way. She decided being single was a good way to avoid further humiliation.

'Come on Daisy, no brooding, that's not why you are here. Time to crack on.'

After clearing away her breakfast dishes, Daisy, with her hands on her hips, stood in the middle of the open-plan kitchen. At the far end was a scrubbed pine table and a two-seater sofa.

The wood burning stove sat back into the chimney breast. The large window let in loads of natural light. Just the place to sit and write.

Re-positioning the table nearer the window allowed Daisy to watch the constant movement in her garden. It was like observing a bird airport, there was so much activity. She delighted at the birds hanging off the feeders, twittering and flying backwards and forwards. Her attention was diverted by a tractor chugging in the field. She couldn't make out who was driving, and wondered if it was Tom.

'Come on Daisy, this isn't going to get you anywhere. Drooling over a fit farmer you have only met once and know nothing about.' An image of being snuggled up in those muscular arms in the depths of winter waved itself before her. Letting out a prolonged sigh, Daisy could easily drift into a daydream.

Shrugging away the images, she opened her laptop and set her mind to the task in hand. Originally, she had written a story called *Rose Water*. It had been about a prince and a princess who lived in entirely separate lands, but both needed the same thing. *The Rose Water*. The only way for them both to survive was to overturn the old ways. This had put them in conflict with each other and caused disharmony between the two realms. Daisy always knew there was more to the characters than she had written and after she was offered a mentorship by Greg, The Rose Water Chronicles evolved.

Her fingers paused over the keys, Daisy felt the familiar shift as she melted away and Alex took over. During the last few weeks, it had become harder to make the transition. The onset of the haunting memories came unbidden and she didn't understand why now, after so many years. It was as if the pain was ignoring her strategy to cope and was ramming her barricade to be free.

'Prince Oritane was besieged by butterflies as he walked the length of the cloisters surrounding his courtyard. They came out of nowhere and fluttered around him, the gentle hum of their wings echoing in his ears. His mother

once told him he was the flame and he drew creatures to him. She also explained he needed to work out how to understand what that meant. Instantly he felt irritated at how often she spoke in riddles to him. He had never understood anything she had said until her untimely death.'

Prince Oritane had started out as a hero, but as Daisy brought him to life, his character developed a mysterious side. Those less sympathetic to the prince mistook this for deceit, calling him the Dark Prince. Oritane knew of the rumours but dismissed them. As he grew older, he realised the importance of playing his cards close to his chest. Little by little, he learned to understand that his dreams were visions and he needed to control and understand them. What Daisy would give right now for a vision into how her current situation was going to end. Not just her own but the prince and princess. She was still grappling to marry his darkness and light and Daisy had to admit she was grappling with her own shadows. Would they dissipate once she had brought peace between the warring factions of Ellodin? A niggle within her intimated it was going to take a bit more than that.

CHAPTER SIX

Checking the time, Daisy was surprised she'd been completely absorbed for over two hours. She pressed save and stood up. Bending to the right and to the left to loosen her muscles, she decided it was time to have a break.

Taking a mug from the cupboard, a noise outside startled her. Spinning round to glance out of the window, a flutter tingled in her tummy. Tom was striding down the garden path carrying something. In sharp contrast to the usual feeling of anxiety building, Daisy felt the flutter increase as Tom tapped on the glass and she waved for him to come in.

'Hi, this is a surprise. Twice in a day.'

Hovering in the doorway, a wide grin spread across his rosy face.

'I thought you might like to try my bees' honey.' His eyes glanced to the table where her laptop was with papers strewn everywhere, then he flicked his head to one side.

'Sorry, I didn't realise you would be working. Most folks come here for a holiday.'

Daisy stepped forward.

'I wish. You caught me out, I'm just making a drink and grabbing a snack. Do fancy anything?'

Oh God, what had she just said?

'I meant anything to eat. Not that I meant I was offering anything else.' The burn on her cheeks spread throughout her whole body. The flutter had grown in size and was in danger of overtaking her. What on earth was the matter with her?

Tom let out a loud gruff laugh.

'You have a way with words Daisy Tremaine, that's a fact. I was literally just passing and thought you might like to try some real honey.'

Clasping her cheeks, wishing the blush would subside, she started to laugh herself.

'There I go, Daisy Babbler. I've been working most of the morning. I definitely need a break.'

An awkwardness rested between them as they continued to stand in the middle of the kitchen.

'What is it you do?'

'Do?'

'Yes, do, as in work? I'm a farmer you are a…?' his lip curled to one side as if he was about to smile.

'Goodness, I don't know what's the matter with me. See I can't even understand what you are saying.' Daisy wasn't sure she wanted to tell him. Her past experiences proved once she told people what she did, they ceased to be interested in her as a person.

'I work for a publishing company. Ooh, is that the honey? It looks yummy. I love honey. Dribbled over bananas is my favourite.'

As Tom handed over the jar, his hand skimmed across hers. A tingling sensation travelled the length of her arm. In an attempt to distract herself, Daisy rolled the glass jar around so she could read the label.

'Weavers Farm honey. Lovingly produced by friendly Weavers Farm bees.' Daisy was amused by the thought of the bees being loving in their production techniques, and by strapping farmer Tom nurturing his bees. Two polar opposites.

'I'd best leave to you to it. Don't want to stop the worker.'

'I do have work I need to finish, but it's such a lovely day, I may venture out into the wilderness for a walk.' Daisy laughed. 'Any recommendations?'

The unease lessening between them, Tom scratched his head.

'See the gate in the fence? Once you are through it, walk in a straight line to the rise and then follow the trampled grass pathway down to the farm. How about you wander over later this afternoon and I'll show you around?'

As their eyes met, Daisy felt goosebumps parade up her arms.

An expectation of hope glistened in Tom's eyes.

'Err, wow, yes I'd love to. If it's not too much trouble? Will the sheep mind me stomping their field?'

'Not a problem. Sheep are quite well behaved. Cows less so if they get spooked. I'd advise sturdy shoes or maybe even boots. Don't worry we have plenty and I think you might be the same size as Tabby.'

Thrown slightly by the reference to her size, Daisy stammered.

'Er, boots, no, walking shoes yes.' Good old Sarah for prompting her to pack a pair.

Tom chuckled well, I'm sure Tabby's should fit you if needed. Mind you, the grounds not too bad. Had a dry spell fortunately. A sweater might be useful. The wind is still a bit sharp. If you are lucky, you might even meet Tabby.'

'Tabby?' Daisy unexpectedly felt an inward disappointment. There was a significant other then. She wasn't sure why this bothered her. They had only just met after all. They knew nothing about each other and she had been less than honest about her work.

'Tabby, short for Tabitha. My errant sister. Owns the horse Bentley who seems to like being at your end of the field.' His thumb indicated the fence where Bentley was standing.

Bewildered by the quelling relief, Daisy beamed.

'Right, sorted, you wander over when you are ready. I'm on admin this afternoon so any excuse to get out of it.' Tom turned to go.

'An excuse, am I?' Daisy started to laugh again, desperate to contain the euphoria flooding through her.

'Can't think of a better one. Well, see you later.'

Stepping outside, she waved to him as he turned to close the gate. Touched by his pause to talk to Bentley and feed him something, she watched as the horse nudged his arm and she heard Tom laugh.

A dreamy sigh emanated from Daisy. What had got into her? She had all the giddiness of a teenager. Her emotions were scattering in the wind. There was one purpose in her life and that was to finish the damn book. Things had been topsy turvy for months now, as much as she tried to deny it. Did she need further complications? There was no denying he was very handsome and charismatic and she had to admit she found it very appealing being an acceptable excuse. The enormity of being on her own came into sharp focus. Was this her life then? Immersed in writing with no chance of anything else? Although having tried anything else it had ended up being a disaster. Sighing, she now conceded that locking herself away didn't seem to be the answer either. Mulling over Tom's invitation, she decided to call Sarah.

'Hey, Daisy, I was just thinking about you,' answered Sarah.

'Ooh spooky. Any reason?'

'I've just been tweaking your website. You've had loads of hits and quite a few encouraging comments. Your readers are eagerly anticipating the third book. How's it going?'

'Yeah, good. I've managed over two hours this morning without any drama. I've settled myself in the snug. It opens out into the kitchen so I can raid the biscuits easier. Plus, the view is amazing. Bit distracting at times.' Gazing out, Daisy thought about the visit to Tom later in the afternoon.

'Ooh sounds a bit cryptic. Anything you want to share?'

'Maybe, I'm just musing.' Daisy pirouetted around the kitchen.

'Daisy, I recognise that tone in your voice. What's going on?'

'Going on? Why do you think there is anything going on?' Daisy stressed the words going on.

'You sound a bit frivolous.'

Daisy began to giggle. 'You will never believe what has happened.'

'I knew it. Out with it. Put me out of my misery.'

'Tom the farmer has invited me for a tour of his farm this afternoon.'

'Get out. Oh my God, Daisy, this is huge news. Tell me more, every tiny detail.'

Daisy spent the next ten minutes filling Sarah in. Aware of the warm fuzzy feeling flowing through her.

'You have been there five minutes and already you have made a hit.' Sarah paused. 'It's fab but please remember why you are there. I would hate for you to suffer more hurt.' The softness of Sarah's voice echoed the thoughts of Daisy.

'I know, I promise to keep myself under strict control.' Daisy couldn't help feeling a little deflated by her friend's reaction.

'Anyway, now you've called I wondered if you fancied company at the weekend?'

'Company?'

'Yes, as in I come and visit you at the weekend.'

'It would be great to see you. I can't recall the last time we spent any downtime together. Text me when you know your plans. Bye.'

Sarah was right, she had been burned before. There was only one thing in her world now and that was the Chronicles. She was distracting herself with Tom so she didn't have to think about anything else. Yet it was so liberating to have something else going on in her life. Feeling slightly dizzy, she sat down and rested her head on the table. Her heart raced slightly and she hovered on the borders of an anxiety build up. Meeting Tom had made her realise how isolated her world was. She was building their meeting up into something it wasn't. Maybe Sarah had a point, she did need to talk to someone. *The trouble was*, thought Daisy, *could she make it through to the end of the book before she took the plunge?*

CHAPTER SEVEN

A soft spring breeze accompanied Daisy as she trekked across the meadow towards Weavers Farm. Occasionally one of the shaggy sheep would lift its head to see what was going on.

Until her visit to the village of Redburn to deliver her talk, Daisy had never given much thought to being part of a rural community. Being a town girl, it felt like everything she needed was on her doorstep. *Not that it had made much difference* thought Daisy. After her mum left, and as she moved into her teenage years, Sarah was always moaning at her for not going out. On a few occasions she gave in but once out, she always wanted to be back home. It felt safer and she could retreat into her writing. As she started writing in earnest, the other girls in her group of friends experimented with make-up, flirted with boys, went on long shopping trips. Daisy had always been on the outside. Not that she made much effort to be on the inside. The library was her biggest haunt. Pondering that episode of her life, Daisy was surprised she harboured some regret. Yet it became a hub of comfort for her as the turmoil of life raged around her.

Quickening her pace, she could just see the roof of a building peeking up as she reached the rise of the field. Daisy could not contain the fizz of excitement growing inside her, eager to take a look at Tom's kingdom. She must be mad with the deadline approaching, going for a tour of a farm! A whisper of guilt glided through her brain. She didn't need to stay long and she did need a break after all.

As the meadow sloped downwards, a collection of barns and finally the full aspect of the house came into view. Daisy halted mid-stride, taking in the scene before her.

Rising up from a sea of yellow and white daffodils, intermixed with tall grasses and lavender, was a sturdy stone-built farm house. Snaking its way across the dark brown stone, a rich red ivy clambered to the roof edge. At the centre of the moss-covered tiled roof were two large red brick chimneys. Beyond that, a winding gravel drive zig zagged into the distance.

Daisy couldn't stop the beaming smile spreading across her face. Strange sensations were pulling her in new directions and she found herself intrigued by where they could take her. She certainly wasn't expecting to see such a grand farm house. Nor feel the building buzz deep inside her at the prospect of seeing Tom again.

Slowly descending towards the house, Daisy walked over a cattle grid and into the garden. A wealth of flowery scents wafted on the warm air. A moment of feeling bewitched by everything around her swept over Daisy.

'Hi, Daisy, you made it.' Startling her, Daisy watched as Tom took long strides towards her.

'Welcome to Weavers Farm.' Spreading his arms wide to emphasise the place he called home. Daisy discreetly cast her eyes over him and noticed he had changed from his work clothes into chocolate cords and a crisp gingham shirt. She couldn't help wondering if he normally changed to do the admin, or if it was for her. Her mind was back in overdrive.

'Tom it's amazing, I'm blown away, it looks as if it's been here forever. I never expected the house to be so grand, so old. That sounds rude, it's just... oh listen, I'm babbling again.'

A throaty laugh filled the air.

'Daisy the babbler strikes again. You're right about its age. It's been in the family a few generations. Come on, let me show you around.'

Without any preamble, he grabbed her hand and a grin filled his face. Suddenly, she had a new sense of liberation sweeping through her. It was intoxicating. Even though they had only just met, it was as if they had known each other for years.

'Let's start outside and then we can head indoors for a drink.'

Daisy allowed herself to be led as Tom gave her the guided tour of various barns and outbuildings, finishing inside a barn which had been converted to a workshop. Mystified by a collection of carved oversized chess pieces, she couldn't stop herself taking a closer look.

'These are stunning. Did you carve them?' Daisy was awed by the intricacy of the workmanship.

Hesitant to reply, Tom stood still. Daisy raised her eyebrows waiting for an answer.

'Yes, I did. I've been interested in wood carving since I was a young lad. It's very soothing... well to me, anyway. Taking a piece of wood from a felled tree and turning it into something other than firewood continues its use long after the tree has died. We had an old chap, Fred, worked here forever. He loved wood, and I loved watching him take the remains of a fallen tree and carve something from it. He taught me everything.'

Daisy was surprised by the depth behind his words. He appeared wistful and momentarily, watching him, she felt a rush of compassion. There was something compelling about Tom, and Daisy knew that whatever was going on inside her crazy brain, she wanted to know more about him.

'Come on, enough dawdling, let's carry on.'

Walking outside, Daisy noticed two long, low buildings towards the end of the drive.

'Does someone live down there?' Daisy pointed to the cottages as they wandered back to the front of the house.

'Not permanently. They are holiday cottages. We converted those a couple of years ago. It was my sister's idea. Before she zoomed off for one of her adventures.'

'Adventures?'

'Tabby has itchy feet syndrome. She speaks several languages and every few months, whoosh, she's gone. She's off shortly to visit the folks in Scotland.' Tom appeared very dismissive.

Daisy stumbled slightly.

'Are you okay?' Tom darted forward to grab Daisy's arm.

Daisy's body trembled as she shook away the instant flashback of her mum bending down to ruffle her hair and kiss her cheek.

'Clumsy feet,' said Daisy, attempting to laugh it off.

'My mum travelled quite a bit when I was growing up. Just reminded me of how she was here one minute, gone the next.'

'I'm parched. It's thirsty work this guiding business. Come on.' Tom held onto her arm, gently guiding her towards the front of the house.

Daisy nodded, a familiar constriction building within her. Please not now, she begged herself. The afternoon had been going so well. Catching her breath, she stilled herself quietly in the hope he wouldn't notice.

The ornately-carved front door opened onto a spacious hall with walls of oak panelling and a grand wooden staircase planted firmly in the centre.

'Gracious Tom, this is something else. Not your average farmhouse, if you don't mind me saying so.'

'There is quite a history to the old place. Rumour has it the staircase was built from oaks which grew on the estate. Let's go through to the kitchen. Hopefully Mrs B has left us a tasty treat.'

Making their way to the kitchen Daisy trailed behind, not wanting to miss anything. Lining the walls were portraits of gentlemen beside horses and women resembling dowager duchesses. All this in a farm house seemed unusual to Daisy, she wondered if they were family or just for decoration.

Entering the kitchen, an aroma of baking greeted her and standing by a large wooden table, enveloped in a bright blue and white apron, was an older lady she assumed was Mrs B.

'You're still here, Mrs B?'

'Just fixing a lunch for Tabby to take with her. I see you and your guest have made it at last. I was beginning to think you had squirrelled her away in that workshop of yours with those damn wood carvings. Hello my dear, I'm Mrs Bowden, generally known as Mrs B. Housekeeper. Sit yourselves down. I've just taken a fruit loaf out of the oven.'

Pulling out a chair, Daisy sat as commanded and was about to reply when Tom cut in.

'As if I would inflict any of my carvings on a new visitor.' Laughter broke out between them and Daisy couldn't help being carried along with the jolliness . A sting caught in her throat as her own family popped into her mind. Granny Jenny was always baking something. Her cherry cake was the best. Daisy recalled how her gran insisted she drop the cherries into the mixture. It had been so long since she had seen her gran. Swallowing back the emotion, Daisy suddenly acknowledged to herself that she had even cut her granny out of her life.

'So, what's it to be? Mrs B makes a great Elderflower lemonade. Fancy giving it a go?'

Tom seated himself next to her and Daisy saw a twinkle of light dancing in his eyes. A pleasurable gush flowed through her. Without warning, her eyes watered and the familiar tears formed. Fidgeting in the hope she could quell them, a queasiness settled within her.

'Hey, it's not that bad.' Tom's arm was around her before she could blink them away.

'I'm such a lightweight. My gran used to bake all the time. I was just thinking how long it is since I've seen her. Memories, they catch you unawares.' Tugging a tissue from her pocket she dabbed her eyes. 'What on earth must you think of me?'

'Tom, fetch the red tin from the pantry. You can't beat a wedge of chocolate cake.' Mrs B bobbed her head towards Tom. Immediately, he was out of his chair and scurrying to the pantry.

'Did I hear you're breaking out the red tin?'

Lifting her face to the sound of a light shrill voice, Daisy's breath caught in her throat as she watched a stunning woman enter the room. Tall and willowy with long sleek black hair, she looked out of place in a working kitchen.

'I swear you have a red tin radar, Tabbs,' Tom said, planting a kiss on her cheek as he walked by her.

'Daisy, meet my errant sister Tabitha, Tabby or Tabbs for short. Tabbs meet Daisy.'

Slightly uncomfortable, Daisy stood up.

'Ah, the famous Daisy? Welcome.' Shaken by the implication of being famous, Daisy mumbled 'hello' and promptly sat down.

'Tabby's idea. A red tin, denoting emergencies when she was

a teenager,' Mrs B announced.

'Few dramas back then, eh Tabbs?' added Tom, winking, trying to prize the lid from the tin.

'Yeah, yeah, but why is it out now?' Tabby asked, plonking herself opposite Daisy.

As the lid came free, Mrs B began dishing out portions large enough to sink a battleship.

'Don't matter why, just enjoy the cake. Right, I'm off.' Mrs B removed her apron and hung it over a chair.

'See you tomorrow, Tom. Don't you fret girl about today, we all have moments in our lives which can spark a few tears.'

As the door closed, Daisy felt Tabby's eyes burning through her.

'Oh, don't tell me, my brother has been boring you literally to tears.'

'Down girl, don't be frightening Daisy on her first visit,' Tom said in a guarded manner.

Daisy put her cake down. The whole atmosphere had instantly become charged with tension.

'Has he been on his soap box yet? His historical tirade about Weavers Farm and the reckless ancestors? He needs a health warning.' Tabby started to laugh. Sitting back in her chair she crossed her long legs and folded her arms.

'Charming as always,' butted in Tom.

Daisy was fascinated by the sibling joshing. She wasn't sure how much was serious but caught a frown on Tom's face. Tabby looked like she was ready to do battle.

'Honestly, he wasn't being boring, it's me. Pollen allergy no doubt.' She took another drink lowering her eyes.

'Anyway,' said Tom, 'that was the illustrious Mrs Bowden. She who is obeyed at all times.'

'She seemed very kind,' answered Daisy, wishing she could be beamed out.

'Don't be fooled. Eh sis, we know the harsh end of Mrs B, don't we?'

'She's a force to be reckoned with, I'll agree,' Tabbs answered, packing her lunch into her bag.

'Right, that's me done, no time to play happy families. I'm off to see the folks.'

'Nice of you to mention it to me. How long this time?' He stood up reluctantly.

Picking her coat from the hook on the door, Tabitha shrugged a shoulder as she tossed her rucksack over the other.

'Tabby, you can't keep doing this you know?'

'No big bro lectures. We all have choices. You've made yours.'

Tabby glanced back at Daisy.

'Lovely to meet you Daisy, sorry it's been short. I'm sure I shall see you again. Don't let my brother rope you into farm jobs. Feel free to ride Bentley, he's a dream.'

Stepping forward to Tom, Tabby wrapped her arms around him.

'Love you too. Stop fussing. I'm fine. I'll text when I get there. Oh, and don't forget the cottages need checking for the visitors due in a week.'

'Tabbs, the cottages are not my responsibility.' Tom's voice became raised as Tabby reached the door. She blew him a kiss.

'Love you too Bro.'

Closing the door behind her, Tom remained still for a moment. Daisy watched as his shoulders sank. What had appeared a warm welcoming kitchen cooled to a chill, causing Daisy to shiver.

'That was Tabby, my unruly miscreant of a sister.' Tom hesitated before speaking, 'I want to show you something.' With that he headed out of the kitchen through the door they had entered earlier.

Daisy was perplexed by what she had just witnessed between Tabby and Tom. Weirdly, an image of her prince flashed through her mind. Was he bewildered? Is that why she was tussling with his next move?

'Are you coming?' she heard him call.

Scurrying after him, she caught him up in a large airy room. Tall windows ran its full length, giving way to a panoramic view of a walled garden.

'Grab a seat,' Tom stretched out a long leg and pushed a small upholstered chair toward Daisy. On a side table she was momentarily distracted by an assortment of family photographs on display.

'I've always loved this room. Originally, it was my father's study and then the library. Hence the wall of books behind you. It's all that's left now. We spent a lot of time in here as children, particularly in winter. The fire would roar up the chimney. Mrs B would plie us with cakes and when no one was around she allowed us to toast marshmallows.'

'Was she your minder, looking after you both? Did both your parents work?'

'Mum didn't work but she had stuff she did, dad worked in London. There were times this family couldn't have functioned without Mrs B.'

Glancing around the room, Daisy noticed how worn everything appeared. The stone surround of the fireplace was darkened where smoke from the fire had been. Despite the height and size of the room, there was a reassuring cosiness that invited you in . She could imagine the antics which had played out here. It must have been a well-loved family home in its day.

'You can see the remnants of the kitchen garden. It was my mother's favourite place. She loved feeding everyone. She and Mrs B were a formidable team once upon a time. We were very self-sufficient here.'

Daisy shuffled on the chair as she stared out to what was an overgrown, neglected space. A sadness settled on her.

'The house was always full of people as we were growing up. Mostly to do with Dad's work.'

Tom was still gazing out of the window.

'Long ago, this was a country estate. Tenant farmers and workers cottages. Plus, the village belonged to the estate. Usual story, an idiot in the family gambled most of it away. Assets had to be sold to pay the debts. By the time it passed to my grandad there was only the farm and a several acres of pasture land left. The Scottish estate, for some reason, was not sacrificed.'

Daisy sat mesmerised, as if she had been transported back into the pages of a history book.

'Back in the day it was known as Weavers Hall. The ancestors were wealthy merchants, making their money in wool and textiles and the mills. When it passed to Grandad, he re-named it Weavers Farm. I get angry with those ancestors of mine. Why would anyone risk all of this?'

'Selfishness? Greed? Wasn't that a time of doffing the cap? Believing they had a right to what they owned. I suppose many of the villagers worked here at one point over the centuries?' Daisy ventured to answer, aware Tom appeared very aggrieved by his ancestors.

'There are still villagers living here who can claim one ancestor or another worked here. Take the cottages near where you are, they were once part of the estate. That's the reason for the gate in your garden'

Daisy warmed to the thought of it being her garden. As a child she had spent long hours in the garden with her mum. Once more memories charged through her brain. She gulped her breath to ward off another stream of tears.

'God, listen to me. Tabby was right, I do pound my chest about the farm.' He sat up and looked at Daisy.

Daisy cleared her throat, tugging at the neck of her sweater.

'You are proud. I get that. Who wouldn't be living in such a fantastic place?'

Uncrossing his legs Tom shifted forward. 'Sorry, I tend to come on a bit strong when I speak about this place. I just love it here. I can't think of anywhere else I'd rather be.'

Fighting back the melancholy seeping through her, Daisy uttered, 'No, I get what you mean. It was kind of you to share it. Home is important. It gives you a sense of belonging.'

'What's your story then Daisy? You mentioned your mum left when you were young.'

Daisy felt the tightening in her chest restricting her ability to breathe. Clutching at her throat, she was shocked when Tom leapt up from his chair.

'Daisy what's wrong?' He leaned over her as she crouched over gasping for breath.

Gently Tom massaged her back, 'It's fine Daisy. You're safe here. Try to slow your breaths. In then out, concentrate on that.'

Mortified at her breakdown, Daisy fought to steady her breathing. She found a degree of comfort in his soothing tone.

After a few minutes Daisy slowly sat upright.

'I'm sorry. You must think I'm crazy. Life's been a bit messy lately. All that talk of family, I think it just got to me.' She sniffed, the tightness receding.

'If you ask me, you just had a panic attack. Tabby has them sometimes when she gets over-stressed. If I rub her back it helps relax her.' Daisy could never have imagined those huge hands being so reassuring and tender. Even more peculiarly, she didn't want him to stop. What was happening to her? A virtual stranger and here he was massaging her back.

'I'll go and grab a glass of water. There's no need to apologise. Take as long as you need to compose yourself.'

Daisy leant back in the chair and closed her eyes. Sarah was right, no more hesitation. She needed to speak to someone about how she could control these attacks. Why on earth would a woman like Tabby, so self-assured and beautiful, have panic attacks? That certainly was a surprise and yet how lovely that her brother cared so much for her that he soothed her.

Tom returned with a glass of water and more cake.

'Better?' he asked as Daisy sipped her drink. She nodded.

'Want to talk about it?'

He held his hand up in a stop gesture, 'Sorry, I don't mean to pry. After all we've only just met.'

Daisy was in two minds how much to tell Tom. 'It's just that if I tell you, things may change.'

'Change? What can you possibly say that would cause anything to change? Unless you are running away from the police?' he chuckled.

'Nothing so exciting, I'm afraid. I'm a writer. My pen name is Alex Dennison.'

'Ah, as in writer of novels?'

Daisy half laughed. 'Yes. It's the reason I'm here. Attempting to finish my final book of a trilogy called *The Rose Water Chronicles*. It's a bit more complicated than that, though.'

'Apologies, I'm not much of a reader. My sister tells me I'm a heathen. However, complicated is nothing new to me.'

Relief flooded through her. There was some consolation in being invisible.

'You're right about the panic attacks. They started a few months ago. They're affecting my work. Embarrassingly, I had one the other day at a presentation. My dad thought a break might help and my friend Sarah thinks I need to see a therapist. I've been trying to ignore them. Denial, I expect a professional would call it.'

'Do you think it's the stress of having to finish the book?'

'Maybe.' Daisy wanted to tell him the whole story but thought better of it. He probably had enough of his own problems and she had only just met him.

'Being here is supposed to help. Therapy is so... I don't know. It's scary. It's like having to admit I'm damaged in some way.'

'Damaged? You're being a bit hard on yourself. From where I'm sitting it can't be any worse than what you just experienced. Especially if it happened whilst you were giving a talk in public. There's a guy in the village, Edward, he was a therapist. I can give you his number.'

Daisy twisted in her seat to look out to the decaying garden. When she had set out earlier, she had felt light and uplifted. The thrill of being somewhere new had given her hope that she could iron out whatever what was going on inside her head. Now, here she was with a man she had only just met and they were discussing her seeing a therapist. This wasn't what she had expected when she had retreated to the back of beyond.

'It's very kind Tom, I don't know. It seems a huge imposition. You appear to have your hands full with your own family.'

'You mean Tabby? Oh, she's always like this. A real drama Queen. I would be more worried if she were not being so dramatic to be honest. I know this is weird, we've only just met. But I would be lying if I said I couldn't care less. There's something about you Daisy, I find I want to get to know you. Apart from anything else, you look like you need a friend and if Ed is willing to help, why not?'

Daisy raised her eyes. How spooky was it that they were both thinking the same? She looked at Tom quizzically.

'I-I don't know what to say, it's all a bit overwhelming. But I'm touched that you care. I'm not sure if I'm ready to share what's really going on. How about you give me this guy's number, I can have a think about it.'

Daisy stood up. The mood had changed and she was flummoxed by Tom's statement.

'Of course, I understand Daisy. I'm not very good at this sort of thing. Give me sheep, horses, my bees and I know exactly what is expected of me. It's just, I sense you are in pain and if I can help then I am happy to do so. One thing about Barley Ford is that we look out for each other, regardless. I'm pleased you made it over this afternoon. Despite everything, I have enjoyed your company.'

Daisy half smiled and nodded, walking over to the door.

'Thank you, Tom. Your animals are lucky to have you.'

With that, Daisy closed the door quietly and found her way back to the outside, wondering if that was how Tom saw her – a wounded animal to be rescued.

CHAPTER EIGHT

Massaging her neck, Daisy could feel her pulse pounding. Sitting opposite the therapist Tom had suggested, she felt like she was in a surreal world. More akin to the ones she wrote about.

'Just to be clear Daisy, I am semi-retired but occasionally I do see clients. Confidentiality is the key in any therapeutic process. In a small place like this you would assume it difficult, but I have yet to be compromised.'

Edward smiled and Daisy was reassured by how it reached his eyes. She hadn't really thought much about confidentiality, but now he mentioned it, she hoped he was true to his word. It was like a guilty secret. Taking a chance on speaking to someone she had never met. Maybe she should change her name to Alice, pretend that she was living in Wonderland, not her home town of Lytton, or Barley Ford, her secret retreat.

'Tom tells me you have only just arrived in the village.'

Daisy thought Edward Thornlee appeared very relaxed and had a calm way about him.

'Yes, about a week now. Tom was kind enough to invite me for a guided tour of the farm. I think I got a bit overwrought.'

Edward nodded. 'Where do you want to begin Daisy?'

'Er, I'm not sure.' I don't get how this works. Never been in therapy before.'

A broad smile beamed out at Daisy.

'Mostly it's you talking, me listening, offering you snippets of things I pick up on. How about you start with what really prompted you to take the leap of faith and see me?'

Daisy chewed her lip.

'There's all this stuff going on. I'm an author and I have a book to finish writing. There's a deadline and it's looming like a dark cloud. My first draft was too weak so I've had to work extra-hard to make it flow. Normally, I don't have a problem, I convinced myself it was writer's block, but then I started having these odd moments where I couldn't breathe and I felt like I was under water. Then there are the dreams I started having around the same time. Actually, they are more like memory flashes.'

Daisy began fiddling with the buttons on her cardigan. It was her comfort blanket. Well beyond its sell-by date. She could feel the tightness rising in her chest.

'Take your time, Daisy, there is no rush. You mentioned dreams, memory flashes?'

'Yes, images to do with my mum. She left when I was ten.' Daisy twisted in her seat.

'I can sense the tension in you. Take a deep breath and let it out slowly.' Edward spoke softly.

Doing as he instructed a couple of times, Daisy began to feel calmer.

'Sounds to me like you are fit to burst with all this stuff.'

Daisy sat bolt upright. 'That's exactly it. I never thought about it like that before.'

'So, now you are thinking about that sensation, can you describe how you feel saying it?'

'Relief, up until now, I've managed to contain everything.'

'Sounds like it's been hard work. It's not easy opening up. I can sense you are uneasy.'

'I guess I am. I'm confused and sad,' Daisy emphasised the word *sad*.

'It's like a wave crashes through me and gets trapped somewhere in here.' She pointed to her heart. 'Can hearts burst with pain and hurt? Can you stop the hurt?'

'Perhaps between us we can find a way to settle the wave and work out why it crashes. As for hearts bursting Daisy, I do believe emotion can be so great that it does indeed feel like a heart could burst.'

'I read somewhere once that when you open a box, you can't squish down the contents and hide them away again. Bit like Pandora's box.'

'That's true. As I said before, you dictate the pace. If it's too much, we stop.'

'Thing is, although Daisy Tremaine is my real name, I've been Alex Dennison since I was nineteen. There are days it is like Daisy has got left behind. The irony being, I write fantasy fiction and I'm beginning to think I've lost touch with my own reality.' Daisy sat back in the seat. 'Do you know I've never thought about it much until now but I can see the similarities between me and Alice in Wonderland.'

Daisy's head drooped. She wasn't sure what to make of it all and part of her worried about Greg or her dad finding out.

'Take your time. This is your story. Opening up I often think is like opening a letter you've held on to, fearing the worst.'

Something shifted invisibly within her and allowed the box lid to lift partially. Straightening herself she knew it was time to face the ghosts.

Aware she had started drifting again, Daisy sighed, staring at the blank computer screen. Her first session with Edward had been nothing like she had imagined. She reflected on how easily she'd been willing to share her anxieties. It was his stillness, which had impressed her. There was an aura about him, an ease which lulled you into thinking you could tell him anything. Even when she started to become edgy, he just gently reassured her, talked her through controlling it. How to take command of the fear and use the energy in a positive way.

Daisy found herself wondering about his existence. Spending your time listening to other people's problems. How on earth did anyone manage to hold all that information? It must be a bit like being a doctor she supposed, you must be able to detach yourself. She wished she could detach herself from the confusion which was beginning to hound her. There was a glimmer of hope that being in therapy would help put things into some kind of order.

Picking up her phone she pressed speed dial for Sarah. It went to her voicemail.

'Hi it's me, just checking in and letting you know the therapy went better than I expected. Call me when you get this.'

Turning back to her laptop she gazed at the screen.

'Urgh! Get a grip Daisy, you need to finish this. You can't leave the prince out there in the dark, the princess needs him. His realm needs him.' Daisy chuckled quietly to herself. As her writing had progressed she'd started speaking aloud to the characters. It gave her a better sense of how they may behave. Right now, she had no idea how they may behave and as if saved by the bell, her phone beeped. A half smile lit her face as she recognised the number, her hands shook a little.

'Tom, hi!' She was still unnerved by his attention.

'Not disturbing you too much am I?' his voiced oozed through the phone.

Twizzling a curl on her finger Daisy carried on smiling.

'I needed a distraction.'

A long, familiar, throaty laugh sent a warm fuzzy feeling through her.

'I was calling to see how it went earlier, with Edward.'

'Amazingly well once I'd calmed down. It wasn't as bad as I thought it would be. I'm seeing him Friday.'

'That's great news. Listen, I have to go over to Weeton Waters in the next hour, do fancy joining me?'

Daisy did a little dance on the spot. It wouldn't take much for her to jump in his Land Rover and enjoy more of his company. Frowning, she knew she was only here for a short time and then what? He was a really lovely guy but what did it all mean? Was there really a connection? The prospect of getting to know one another better? Isn't that what he'd said to her?

'Daisy, are you there?'

'Yes, yes. I was trying to decide if I could spare the time but you know, I really need to get on. It's a lovely idea and I would love to, but my agent Greg is calling me later for an update. Maybe another time?' Would he ask her again?

'Heh that's not a problem, it was just an idea. I'll leave you to it and good luck with the work call. Take care. Glad this morning wasn't too bad. Maybe we can catch up later.'

With that the phone went dead and Daisy flopped onto the chair. Letting out a long moan, timing was everything, just her luck to finally meet someone she connected with. Yet here she was stuck with deadlines and the past crowding in on her. What was it he had said? He was better with animals, he recognised when an animal was in distress and had a need to save them. Disappointment flooded her as Sarah's words floated in her head. 'Remember why you are there.' Daisy knew she was acting like a lovesick teenager. Who was she kidding? If she didn't finish this blessed book, she would have less of a life than she had now.

Lifting her head, she brought her laptop back to life.

'Come on Prince Oritane, let's get you some action, cos boy we could use some.'

CHAPTER NINE

After a long afternoon of writing, Daisy yawned and, noticing the light outside changing, she switched off her laptop. Not moving for a few moments, she knew she always had to give herself time to re-orientate back into the present. Breaking the silence, her phone beeped. Her heart sank a little seeing the caller's name. Taking a deep breath, she pressed accept.

'Greg, hi.'

'Daisy, is this a good time?'

Shaking her head and mouthing no at the phone, she coolly pronounced it was.

'I've read the latest draft and yeah, you are back on track. Country hideaways must be good for you. Any chance I can have the rest of the manuscript by the end of the week?'

'This week? No, I'm not sure I'm that far on Greg.' A surge of nausea swirled around in Daisy's stomach.

Greg burst out laughing, 'Worth a try. Seriously, I'm liking where you are taking things.'

'Fresh surroundings and very few interruptions. I suppose it is having an effect. Thank goodness, I was getting a bit worried.' Daisy wandered through to the lounge at the front of the cottage.

'No need to worry, I had every faith in you. Just seems to have taken a while for you to get into your groove with this one. So, what's it like where you're staying? You haven't said much.'

Distracted by seeing Gerald, Daisy waved and grinned as he waved back.

'Daisy? You've dropped out... I can't hear you.' An urgency sounded in Greg's voice.

'No, I'm still here. Very peaceful. Funny, I can only describe it as soothing. Greg, I just wanted to say I appreciate your patience. Things had got a bit on top of me. It feels like a big moment finishing the chronicles. I have to admit, it's made me wonder what comes next.'

It was Greg's turn to go quiet. Daisy sat down, fearful of what he was going to say.

'I don't think you need to be concerned on that score. I think you will find there'll be plenty going on. I wasn't going to mention anything yet, but I may have news later this week... so you carry on and get those words out of your head and onto the paper. Complete focus, Daisy.'

'News? What do you mean?'

'Nothing dreadful, I assure you. Quite the opposite. I shouldn't have said anything. Keep writing, Daisy, let the words stream onto the page. I have to go. Email me the next few chapters you finish. Take care. Bye.'

Daisy wondered what on earth the news could be. She wasn't sure she could face another book about Ellodin.

A sharp tap on the window made Daisy jump. Looking up, she saw the cheery face of Dorothy peering through the glass. Opening the window, Daisy was surprised how pleased she was to see her.

'Grab your coat and join us for a stroll. It's such a beautiful evening, shame to waste it indoors.' Dorothy had an insistence in her tone that Daisy could hardly argue with.

'Of course. Give me a couple of minutes.' Glad of another distraction, Daisy pulled on her jacket and wrapped her scarf around her neck. It was still chilly even though spring was beckoning.

Within minutes she was striding down the lane with Dorothy, Harry eagerly sniffing the hedgerows for rabbits.

'Have you lived here long Dorothy?' Daisy asked, keeping her eyes on the track ahead. She had the impression Dorothy wasn't keen on sharing.

'A number of years. After a while you stop counting.'

'It seems an unlikely place to end up. It's so far off the beaten track. It strikes me you would have to have visited on holiday, or know someone in the village to actually decide to move here.'

'I can see why you would think that.'

Kicking the stones in front of her, Daisy knew when she had been fobbed off.

Having reached the river, Dorothy stopped.

'Let's sit a while, shall we? Harry and I don't do walking without stopping these days.'

The two women found a large rock to perch on.

'Anyway, how are you doing? Settling in nicely? Such a lovely little cottage. I nearly bought it myself when it came up for sale. But then I do love where I am, so I changed my mind. Familiarity becomes important the older one gets.'

'I can't believe how easily I have installed myself. It's so cosy and inviting. It was my dad's idea to have a break.' Daisy swallowed, uncertain why she had said that.

Dorothy bent down and picked up a stone, turning it over in her hand before launching it into the river.

'That doesn't surprise me. You reminded me of a rabbit stunned by the headlights that first day.'

Daisy was somewhat perturbed by Dorothy's perception of her.

'Really, oh my goodness. Did I? I guess I was a bit lost when I came here. It's an odd place, Barley Ford. It has an almost bewitching atmosphere, like you are being held in time. You'll think I'm mad, but I keep expecting mist to come down and the whole place to disappear.'

Dorothy turned to Daisy.

'Barley Ford is unusual, I agree. There's a lot of history attached to the place. It was part of a larger estate centuries ago. I'm sure Tom has told you that story already. Sadly, parts have been sold off over the years. The village remains much as it was, a few new cottages but for the most part, if you stepped back in time, I'm not sure that much would be different.'

'How did you end up here?' Daisy was never one to give up.

Dorothy gave a little laugh and fed Harry a treat.

'Ah. That, my dear Daisy, is a story for another time.'

Dorothy took hold of Daisy's hand. Slightly alarmed, Daisy held her breath as her companion stroked it.

'I can see pain in your eyes, Daisy. Those eyes are searching for answers. Barley Ford holds many souls who have searched for answers. The answers often lie within us. This remote little village is the sanctuary which allows us the space to explore.'

Daisy shivered, captivated by Dorothy's words. A little unnerved by her observations, she briefly wondered if Dorothy was a modern-day witch. Her skin was flawless and even though her eyes had a watery glaze, they still sparkled. There was an aura of otherworldliness; a sense of knowing. Daisy momentarily drifted to Ellodin and the prince's mother.

'You are very insightful Dorothy. There are things I have shut away. I'm beginning to appreciate that I need to address them before they ruin me.'

Staring out across the river, Daisy astonished herself with this admission. It was true, for all these years the memories of her mum had been securely locked in a vault. If she didn't get herself sorted out, she would never finish the book. Yet it was more than that. If she didn't take control of her life, she would never have one. Little by little, she sensed chinks of light peeking through the darkness she often found herself in.

Continuing to hold Daisy's hand, Dorothy continued. 'You asked what brought me here. Life brought me here. Yet, in the end, I, myself, kept me here. Mostly because I was stubborn about forgiving. My brother declared me a modern-day hermit.'

'Do you regret staying?'

Letting go of her hand, Dorothy picked up another stone and stared at it, rubbing the edges of it with her thumb.

'Regret is a waste of energy. Better to re-direct it. We all have a past, sometimes dwelling on it can be toxic. You cannot undo what has been. A little birdie tells me you have met our illustrious professor.'

Daisy altered her position on the rock. She too had a past, but was starting to realise that it was full of holes. She wished her dad had been more open about her mum and the reasons she left and never stayed in touch.

'Professor? Do you have a professor in the village?'

'Oh yes, Edward Thornlee. He ended up here too. Who knows Daisy, maybe you will end up here as well? Come along Harry, let's head back. You coming Daisy?'

Daisy was shocked at Dorothy's candour.

'How did you know I'd seen Ed?' Standing up, Daisy rubbed the backs of her legs. Please don't let it be Tom.

'There are few things which happen here that don't go unnoticed. Don't look so worried, Gerald is like a sentry in the village. There is nothing he doesn't miss. He's the kind of man who has your back when you need someone. Very serene, for a man. Tom is a good man too Daisy. He has a lot on his plate. A devoted farmer who believes passionately about the survival of the countryside. He carries the weight of his inheritance very seriously. Sometimes too much, I fear.'

Dorothy held out her hand for Daisy to help her up.

'Interesting that you refer to him as Ed. I haven't heard him called that in a very long time. Come on Harry, time for supper.'

Walking ahead, Dorothy left Daisy standing, gazing out across the water. She wasn't sure what to make of what Dorothy had said. It spooked her. Daisy realised she referred to Edward as Ed quite a bit in her head. It seemed more apt to his personality. Edward seemed a very remote part of him. This visit was becoming stranger and stranger. Slowly turning, she watched Dorothy chatter away to Harry. Now if Harry was a black cat, that would just about floor her.

'I swear, Sarah, Dorothy is some kind of modern-day witch. She has this ability to be ultra-perceptive, it's spooky. Maybe she was in the police. This place is very unnerving.'

Catching up with Sarah was Daisy's favourite part of the day, no matter how late it was. Curled up in bed, Daisy had spent the last ten minutes relaying the events of the afternoon.

'She sounds eccentric but lovely. Keeping an eye on you by the sounds of it. I wondered if you had thought anymore about me coming over?'

'Yes, I have and if you promise to give me space to write in the mornings, we can have the afternoons.'

'Brilliant, I'll be over lunchtime Friday. You can introduce me to all the delights of Barley Ford.' Sarah burst out laughing.

'Sarah Billingham, you are dreadful.'

CHAPTER TEN

Groaning as she slowly opened her eyes, Daisy's head throbbed. She buried her face in the pillow, hoping it would take away the feeling that someone had pummelled it like a blob of bread dough. Faces had been drifting around in her dreams, with nonsensical words streaming out of their mouths.

At one point she had imagined hearing her mum singing. Rolling over, she watched streams of sunlight glide across the ceiling. It had become her morning ritual to follow the progression of the early morning sun in her room. Today though, she was caught in a web of memories. Rather than fight the tears, she let them slide down her cheeks. Ed had explained that tears were a release of emotion and to suppress them suppressed the emotion. Although with the amount of crying she had done, she should be all out of emotion.

Stepping back to view her life, she felt like she was trapped in some sort of parallel universe; surrounded by those she knew and loved, but living a totally different life to them. Even her writing ceased to bring her the joy it once did.

Yesterday, when she had been talking to Dorothy, Daisy had become aware of how many things around her parent's separation were vague. Her dad was still acting evasively when she spoke to him. She was becoming more convinced he was holding something back. Why did her mum just up and leave like that? She knew they had argued. Her dad had admitted that much. Yet he refused to divorce her, why?

Reluctantly pushing the covers back, she slid out of bed and went through her daily routine on autopilot. Tears still prickled at the back of her eyes and she fought to keep them away. But they came unbidden and as fast as she wiped them away, more stacked up behind. When would it all stop?

Checking her clock, she knew she needed to get a move on if she was to make Ed's appointment. She found herself looking forward to it. Oh God, was this what she was reduced to? Looking forward to a therapy session.

Although she wasn't hungry, she forced herself to have a breakfast bar and glugged some milk form the carton. Granny Jenny would not have approved at all. This raised a smile and Daisy knew she must call her. It had been too long. She wondered if Granny Jenny knew anything about Mum. After all, she was her daughter. Shaking her head at the complications littering her life, she picked up her phone and bag and banged the door behind her.

'Good to see you, Daisy. You look a bit washed out. Not sleeping?'

Daisy shuffled in the chair. 'Not last night. Endless nonsensical dreams. Today, I'm inert.'

'Not completely, you've moved enough to get here. You have traces of milk on your chin, so you've eaten or drank.'

'God who are you, Sherlock Holmes?'

'A keen observer, it's not all about the talking. As a writer you must recognise that observation is everything.'

'Fair point.'

'How are you feeling after our last session?'

'I've burst. The cereal packet has well and truly spread its contents all over the frigging floor. How am I ever going to sweep them up?'

'Do you want to sweep them up?'

'Yes, I do. I want to be able to function like a normal human being again. I don't want to feel out of control the way I do when I go into panic mode.'

'That's a good step forward. You want change?'

'I've been thinking about the prince in my book. In this last adventure, he has to complete the quest to bring home the Rose Crystal. What if he can't do it?'

Ed re-positioned himself, taking a moment to consider her question.

'It's your story. What do you want him to do?'
Without hesitation, Daisy fired right back at Ed.
'He's the hero. He has to make it, right? Good has to prevail.'
'There's your answer then.'
Daisy sighed, tugging at her sleeve.
Ed continued: 'He's found himself in tough situations. Some are of his own making, true, but now he has met Princess Lilia, there is hope.'
Daisy shot up in her seat.
'You've read my books?'
'Not completely, my curiosity was piqued so I looked them up online and read some extracts. In reality, rather than fiction, there is a belief that it's no coincidence we cross paths with certain people in our lives. In your world of the prince and the prophecies he grew up with, he was clearly meant to meet the princess in order to find hope; to rescue and recover his kingdom. I wonder if this is how you see your own path?'
Daisy leant forward rubbing her forehead.
'Deep down I know I've struggled to manage. I didn't want to admit it though. At first, I put it down to the stress of finishing the book. The nearer I get to the end of the book, the more the memories of my mum are flashing through my brain. Since coming here, talking to you, it's dawned on me that I have no idea why she left. When I talk to my dad, he is ultra-evasive. I've even wondered if she's dead and he hasn't had the courage to tell me. Even my Granny Jenny, who I haven't seen in an age... she's my mum's mum, so what does she know? I do know that I have been in hiding, and now I have put my head above the parapet I can see things I refused to see before.'
Allowing the moments to tick by, Ed gave Daisy the time to consider what she had just said.
'That's a big admission. We all engineer a strategy to hide. It's how we protect ourselves.'
A stillness settled between them.
'Tell me about your mum.'
Pulling at her scarf, Daisy knew she could no longer squash

things behind the walls she had built. A familiar quiver resonated deep in her chest. Breathing in deeply and attempting to steady herself, she carried on.

'Mum was always jetting off somewhere. She was a civilian attached to the military. Dad used to tell me she was a people person, and lots of people needed her skills. I never understood what that meant. When I was ten, she jetted off and never came back.'

Edward leaned forward. 'Those are facts. They don't tell me anything about her.'

Daisy stared at him. She noticed he had flecks of green in his grey eyes. They were enquiring eyes, full of expression. They held you, urging you to go further.

'At age ten you will have memories of her...'

Daisy hesitated, knowing if she started speaking about her mum, the quiver in her chest would intensify. And yet she knew she had to try. Jiggling her legs up and down, it was as if she was about to do a high dive.

'Laughter, she was always laughing. When she had been away, she always brought home something as a memento. A fridge magnet, a postcard, a tacky touristy gift of where she had been. Once she brought this hideous troll. She said it had reminded her of Dad when he was grumpy. She giggled every time she looked at it.'

A grin played across Daisy's mouth. She had forgotten about the troll. She wondered where it was now. The fridge magnets were still where she had left them, littering the door of the fridge.

'When she was home, she was always planning things for us to do. Dad used to get irritated because he would be locked away in his study and Mum would barge in and wrap her arms around him and do this daft cooing noise. I can hear her whispering to him, urging him to put away his work. He capitulated every time. She was very persuasive.'

Daisy had not thought about any of this for years. All these memories had been securely locked away. Sadness began to weave through her.

'After the way things were at home, what could have been so horrific that she needed to leave?' Daisy sniffed away the hurt, the abandonment.

'There are many reasons why mothers leave their children. In my experience, it's never done lightly,' Edward offered. 'You've never asked your father why?'

'I may have done in the early days. He was always checking up on me to make sure I was okay. I would ask him then about why she left, but he dodged the questions. Even before I came away, I broached the subject again, it was Sarah really who told me I should. It didn't do any good, he evaded the subject and told me to focus on the book.'

Daisy stared into space before carrying on.

'I remember this one, blustery October day, it was after school and Mum took me to the park for a picnic. It was crazy, everything was blowing everywhere, and we just laughed. Funny, I can remember how much fun she was. Then, there was this time, I pestered her to sleep outside and she let me, but on the condition that she shared the tent. We lay there for ages and looked up at the stars.'

'Your memories are spilling out now, Daisy. When was the last time you recalled all these things? There is such a fondness in your recall.'

'I miss her. Every day.' Daisy's lips trembled. 'Why did she leave? Where she is now?'

Leaning further forward, Ed's voice was barely above a whisper. 'Do you want to find her, Daisy?'

Twizzling the hooped earring she was wearing, Daisy screwed up her face and nodded.

'Is it time you and your dad had a real conversation? It must have been painful for him, too. His wife left him as well...'

Ed was right; she had never considered her dad in all of this. At the heart of all this was her need for answers.

'My dad's been amazing I can't take that away from him. Maybe it's been easier to believe she didn't care, then I wouldn't have to think too much about it. I agree though, women do inexplicable things to protect those they love. The thing is, just now, it's so important to write. I need to get my prince back into the light, and Princess Lilia into his castle... and maybe even his bed. I can't do it. They won't do as I bid them. It's so frustrating.'

Daisy clenched her fists and shook her head, anger suddenly tearing her through her.

'Daisy, have you thought about letting go of the prince and princess to see where it takes them? Hand over the control to them, rather than drive yourself to provide their answers.'

Lifting her head up, Daisy narrowed her eyes.

'What do you mean? I write the words.'

'Yes, you do, but it strikes me that from the things you have told me, usually you are led by their actions. Whereas now you are trying to lead them.'

Daisy rubbed her eyes. He had a good point. She was trying to force herself to get to the end.

'As for your mother, in my experience, the choices before us are often so limited that the action outweighs the consequence. Whatever the reason for your mother leaving, it must have been quite something.'

Edward checked his watch and stood up. 'Why don't we call it time? I think you have plenty to consider.'

Daisy nodded as she stood up. Momentarily, she recalled Dorothy telling her Gerald was a sentry. Looking at Ed now she thought he was a sentinel of people's minds. He was quite tall and she noticed how his hair fell forward over his face, but he didn't push it away like Gerald was prone to do.

'I've never shared any of this with anyone. I'm not sure how you do this, get people to open up, but thank you. Maybe I need to take it from here. You've helped me slide into the light. Now I need to slide my prince into the light. You have a point about the characters.'

'Call me if you need to talk again. Good luck with the story Daisy, these things have a way of working out.'

Walking away from Ed's cottage, Daisy agreed, there was heaps to think about. Not least the ending of the book.

CHAPTER ELEVEN

There were moments of her life which Daisy cherished. Moments she had not hidden away. Like the time she won a poetry competition at school. Nervously, she had climbed the few steps onto the stage to accept the award. She could still recall the heaviness squatting in her chest, wishing her mum had been there to see her. As Daisy thanked the headmistress, she had turned to the audience to read out the poem. Staring at the page, the words all became jumbled and then she heard a voice call out.

'Chin up, Daisy, you can do it.'

Staring out into the sea of faces she spotted her mum standing up, egging her on. The heaviness emptied and joy took over. Seeing her mum meant more to Daisy than receiving the prize.

It was a very rare occasion her mum was present. Mostly, it had been her dad, because her mum was always somewhere else. There was always an air of mystery to where. Except when she wasn't there, the house was empty of laughter. Some days, her dad would wander around like a lost soul; there were days he wouldn't even shave. Odd memories were starting to scatter through her mind like April showers. Ed had mentioned people often found a way to block out pain. She was beginning to accept she had spent hours writing stories with happy endings because she longed for her own. It still troubled her to delve into the memories that were surfacing, but if she was going to get through this, she needed to break down her walls.

Aware she had started drifting again, Daisy sighed, staring at the blank computer screen.

'Urgh! Why won't the words come? You can't leave the prince out there in the dark, the princess needs him. His realm needs him.'

Perhaps Ed had been onto something when he suggested letting go. Was she trying too hard to force things?

Taking a deep breath and closing her eyes, she pictured the prince in his garden.

'Okay Prince, what are you thinking, what are you feeling?'

Daisy chuckled quietly; if anyone was listening in, they would think she was mad. She had developed this way of working early on in her writing. Talking to the characters made them real and gave her a better sense of how they may behave. If she was the princess, she would have kicked the prince's ass by now, but where was the fun in that happening straightaway? It was true she had done less talking to the characters recently. Overthinking what was to come rather than what was in the moment.

Her phone buzzed. Relieved to have a good reason to stop working, she answered.

'Hi, Dad.' Although pleased to hear from him, Daisy had the impression they were skating on thin ice together.

'Just checking in. See how you are doing?'

'Surprisingly, I'm making headway.' She answered in a clipped tone.

'Great, how are you finding Barley Ford?'

'It's beautiful and wild and just what I needed.' Daisy stared out of the window, watching a flock of birds fly over. 'Dorothy Swift is amazing, the lady you booked the cottage through.'

'She sounded very business-like on the phone. I wondered if it would be too quiet.'

'On the contrary Dad, it's a hive of intrigue. Dorothy is lovely. I think she's keeping me under a watchful gaze. How's you?'

'Busy, new project on the horizon. Remember Charlie Henderson. I worked with him a lot in the old days?'

'Of course I remember Charlie, he was always turning up claiming his wife never fed him and had hidden his whiskey.'

Dan burst out laughing.

'Yeah, he did, didn't he? I'd forgotten that, well not so much pinching my whiskey. He's thinking of writing a book about his experiences as a travel journalist. He's asked if I fancy co-writing.'

'That's fantastic news. Sounds like it's a great project. You are going to say yes?'

'I'm considering it. Collaborations can be tricky and I think I need to know more about his ideas first.'

Before Daisy could reply, her dad continued.

'Hopefully you are sleeping better, given what you told me about your dreams.'

Daisy's shoulders sagged.

'Daisy?'

'Dad, there's something I need to tell you. Please don't flip but I'm seeing a therapist. Here in Barley Ford. He's semi-retired, but agreed to see me. He knows Tom. It's helping.'

'A therapist? In the village? Who is Tom?'

'Sorry I thought I had mentioned him. He owns the farm and land that backs onto my garden here. He's been…' *Warm, kind, distracting, a breath of fresh air in my stilted life*, thought Daisy.

'He recommended Edward, although I've taken to calling him Ed for some reason. Tom's sister has seen him apparently. Sarah was right, I need to work through things.'

Daisy tried to imagine the expression on her dad's face.

'That's a surprise.'

The tone in her dad's voice altered slightly.

'He's semi-retired. A professor.'

'A professor?'

'Yes. He's still able to practice even though he's semi-retired.'

'Is it helping, talking to him?'

'Yes, surprisingly. I haven't told Greg. Not sure he'd want this getting out to my fan base. Anyway, I feel calmer. I'm writing with more of a flow.'

'I'm glad, Daisy. Perhaps you just had a bit of writer's block after all.'

Daisy didn't silence the groan she let out. 'No, I think it has been much more than that, Dad. I know you hate talking about Mum, but Ed thinks it may help if we have a proper conversation about what happened.'

'Oh, does he? I've told you it was a long time ago and there is no point in dragging it all up again.'

'That is the point though. We have never talked, discussed it. You have always skated over it. Almost believing one day she'll just turn up. Why dad, why do you think that?'

'Daisy, Daisy.'

'What? Look if you are not willing to help, I need to get on. Love you, Dad.'

'Daisy, please, let's not fight over this.'

'I'm not fighting you. I just need some answers and you are the one dragging his heels. I love you, Dad, but you are driving me crazy.'

Daisy could picture him at the other end, rubbing his forehead as he often did when he was frustrated.

'I need to go. Love you Daisy button. Keep in touch.'

Daisy threw her phone onto the table. He was so infuriating. She was more convinced than ever that he was hiding something. There was a part of the puzzle he was keeping to himself. It was so frustrating.

Despite all the distractions of Tom, Dorothy, even seeing Ed (and why had she suddenly started calling him Ed?), there was no escaping the bleak reality of how much she missed her mother. Lost in the familiar sadness wrapping its arms around her, Daisy closed her eyes.

'Prince Oritane was besieged by butterflies as he walked the cloisters of his courtyard. They came out of nowhere and fluttered around him like moths to a flame. His mother once told him, he was the flame and others fanned it. He had never understood what she meant until her untimely death.'

Daisy snapped her eyes open and sat up suddenly. Butterflies! That's it! Prince Oritane had started out as a hero. Bringing him to life, she had created a character who was vulnerable and trusting. But there was an air about him, a mystery. DPAs he grew, he understood the suspected darkness was caused by his dreams. As they evolved, he realised they were visions. Meeting the princess had opened his heart and his confidence had grown as he understood his destiny was in his own hands.

It's human nature to judge, to make an assumption about a person, a situation without fully knowing the backstory. That was it, that was the key, the back story!

Flipping open her laptop, a surge of energy rushed through her and she bristled with excitement.

In the final book she was grappling to marry his darkness and light; interweave into his story the reasons why. The struggle to bring him home, to show him the light was all around. Daisy needed to get him into the light – and the princess off her high horse.

CHAPTER TWELVE

Daisy's elation from the previous day had led to her working late into the night and sleeping in. Her own shadows were still hovering at the edges, but the ending was close, and she felt something similar to fear at the prospect of reaching it. Nevertheless, she wanted to celebrate turning a corner with the book. On the spur of the moment, she had called Tom late that afternoon, inviting him to dinner. She wasn't sure what prompted her rash decision except gratitude for the kindness he had shown her . A tingle of excitement flooded through her when he had accepted. She couldn't recall the last time she had cooked for someone else.

Chopping the ingredients for the chicken curry, Daisy found herself thinking that she knew very little about Tom the person. She understood his intensity about the farm: it was his passion it drove him to get up each morning. But what intrigued her the most was the familiarity between them. Within hours of being together and her embarrassing meltdown, he had suggested someone who could help her. Daisy was beginning to understand how this community operated. They genuinely did look out for one another. Dorothy seemed to think highly of Tom but had commented that he had a lot going on. Families, Daisy decided, were complicated. Giggling, she allowed herself to think about Tom's ruggedness and down-to-earth charm. She couldn't help but wonder what it would be like to be enveloped in those muscular arms.

A loud rap on the door ended the image abruptly. Spinning round, Daisy saw the door open, and Tom walked through.

'Evening, not too early?'

Daisy's heart fluttered as she drank in the vision before her. He had made a visible effort to dress for the evening with a crisp looking pale blue shirt and dark grey chinos. Such a change from how she had become used to seeing him. With the back of her hand, she brushed her hair from her face. A familiar blush travelled across her cheeks.

'Hi! No, please come in. Ooh is that a bottle?'

'Mind what you are doing with that knife.'

'Ooops,' Daisy placed it on the chopping board.

'Actually, it's wine for you and beer for me.' Tom held up a couple of cans. 'I'm not much of a wine drinker.'

Goosebumps prickled her skin. Every time she was in his company she lost all sense of holding herself together. What on earth was happening to her?

'I'm just finishing things off. Please, take a seat.' Turning her attentions back to boiling the rice, Daisy was aware of the rising heat in the kitchen.

Finally seated at the table, Daisy served the curry, feeling relieved at the relaxed yet intimate atmosphere. Tom was pouring her a glass of wine and music played in the background. It was as if they did this all time. *Steady, girl*, she thought, *this is just dinner, a thank you for his help.*

'This looks magnificent Daisy. Thank you.'

Regaining her composure, Daisy took a sip of wine.

'I wanted to thank you for being so kind since I arrived. Introducing me to Edward has been a great help. Hate to say it, but Sarah was right, I did need to talk to someone. I can be extremely stubborn. Not sure it's impressed my dad though.' Picking at her food, she wondered if she was ever going to be able to eat it.

'Ed is a hero of Tabby's. She swears he has some sort of superpower and can see right inside your brain.' Tom put a fork full of curry into his mouth. Pointing his fork at his dish, he gave a thumbs up with his free hand.

'This is delicious.'

'Curry is my go-to dish. I learned to cook it in the early days of Dad and I being on our own. He was always calling the local takeaway. It didn't seem healthy. Glad you are enjoying it.'

'Must have been hard on him, trying to cope as a single dad.'

'I guess. To be honest I hadn't really given it much thought until recently. When I was growing up, I suppose we just got on with things. My gran used to come round, but then she stopped.' Daisy had another sip of wine. Not wanting to remember the loneliness of being left twice.

Tom put his fork down and reached out, laying his hand over hers. 'I have no idea what things must have been like, but it sounds lonely.'

She stared at the giant hand covering her own. A tremor started somewhere deep inside her.

'Yes, it was. I think that is why I started writing. Living in make-believe worlds seemed easier.' She eased her hand away.

'A chef and a writer. Great combination. I don't know what I expected a writer to be like, but I never imagined someone like yourself.'

Daisy laughed, 'Should I ask what you did have in mind?'

'That didn't come out right. I don't know what I meant really. I've only ever read a couple of crime stories. I don't really know what you write about. Still, who knows, with a little persuasion maybe I can be converted to a reader.' His eyes twinkled as he looked across the table at Daisy.

Daisy almost choked on her food. There was no denying their growing connection and the ease of their friendship. Yet here he was, openly flirting. Touching her skin as if he did it every day. A shared intimacy she had never suspected could grow so quickly.

Pouring herself another glass of wine for Dutch courage, she took a deep breath.

'When I tell people what I do it sometimes has an adverse effect.

Tom lay his fork on the side of the plate and picked up his beer.

'In what way?'

Daisy melted as a smile spread across his face and lit up his deep syrupy eyes.

'Often people are more interested in the perks of me being a writer, not me personally. I suppose over the years I've built a wall around me.'

Tom started to grin, 'Well in my experience, walls can be taken apart stone by stone. How I see it is that a panic attack is no perk. Nothing you tell me could change the dreams I've been having.' Tom held her gaze.

Suspended in the charged atmosphere, Daisy and Tom regarded one another. Small pin prick explosions pierced her hand, travelling up her arm. Something was happening that she had no control over. It was like being held in a spell. They had only just met and yet there was so much energy charging around them, she was in danger of self-igniting. If she was honest with herself, it was a little terrifying.

Putting her cutlery to one side, she sat back in her chair.

'Wow, I'm flattered Tom. I'm not sure I know what to say. Until I came here, I hadn't realised how much of a bubble I have been living in. Maybe it's time to fill in a few gaps.'

Leaning back in his chair and putting his hands behind his head, Tom nodded.

'Explain away.'

'Nineteen years ago, my mum walked out on me and Dad with no explanation. They had a big row the night my dad was due to go to an award ceremony. He's a travel writer and was at the height of his career. I was used to her coming and going as she worked for the army, in a civilian capacity. This time was different because Dad was evasive about where she was and when she would return. After a month, Dad still hadn't told me when she would be back. That month turned into two, then three. By then I had got used to her being away and Dad and I became the norm. Eventually, Dad sat me down and told me she wouldn't be coming back. He had tried to keep working, but it became impossible. So his work became more freelance and he made me his priority.'

Pausing to gauge Tom's reaction, Daisy shifted in her seat.

Tom nodded, urging her to continue.

'Writing became my comfort blanket. It's something I've always done since I was a young child. Mum would sit and listen to all my stories, encouraging me.'

Daisy blinked away the tears. How could she have forgotten the delight her mum displayed when she read to her?

'At the age of eighteen I entered a writing competition and was runner up. On the back of that I was offered the chance to develop my story and now, more than a decade later, I am known as Alex Dennison, author of *The Rose Water Chronicles*. Then, several months ago, I started having these fractured images of my mum. And the pain I thought I had buried started to re-emerge.'

Tom was about to speak but Daisy shook her head. This was difficult and she didn't want to stop, fearful she wouldn't be able to carry on.

'My best friend Sarah became my assistant, looking after my webpage and blog and helping out with book signings. After I had the weird episode at the talk I was giving, Sarah instantly knew something was wrong. It was her idea for me to speak to a professional. Or to take some time out with no distractions to finish the book. To be fair, I chickened out and chose finishing the book. It scared me though. My editor Greg has sent my draft back twice. I couldn't even construct a sentence. The tipping point was the presentation, followed by my dad telling me to take some time out and concentrate on finishing the book. He suggested I come here.'

Tom had become statuesque whilst he listened to Daisy recount her tale.

'Thanks to Ed – sorry, Edward – my head is clearing and the words are finding their way back onto the page. However, I've discovered there are a lot of unanswered questions between my dad and I have for my dad. One step at a time though. Finish the book.'

Tom exhaled a long breath.

'I wasn't expecting that. Parents, they sure mix things up, I know that. My own had their moments. For me, it was my dad who was absent most of the time. He worked in London. Then suddenly, out of the blue, he would appear with a load of people. Mum was expected to feed and find beds for them. Her comfort was the garden. She worked her frustrations out on the weeds.'

Tom took a swig of his beer before returning to the present.

'That first day you visited, you mentioned your granny, was that some sort of trigger?'

'Mrs B reminded me of my Granny Jenny, my mum's mum. She looked after us when Mum walked out. Then she left. Dad said it was too much for her. I suppose that it was around the same time that writing became my escape, a way of protecting myself against anyone else leaving. The trouble is that I barricaded myself into my world and isolated myself from my friends. Sarah was the only one who managed to storm my fortress.'

Daisy dropped her head into her hands as the tears came silently unbidden. It was draining explaining it all to Tom. Yet it had been strangely cathartic.

Slowly, rising from the table, Tom went to Daisy and pulled her up from her seat. She rested her head on his shoulder.

Without warning, he gathered her up in his arms and carried her through to the lounge. Cradling her in his arms, he carefully laid her on the sofa, then sitting beside her, he held her hand until the tears subsided.

Daisy thought her heart was going to burst, it was pounding so much.

Hesitantly, she turned her face to him and asked, 'You don't mind, then? Me being a crazed writer in therapy?'

Brushing a tear from her cheek, Tom lowered his head and gently grazed Daisy's lips with his own.

'Is that answer enough?'

A warm flush of contentment flowed through Daisy. In awe of the new sensations invading her very core, she uncurled herself from him. Trembling, she took Tom's hand in her own and gently pulled him to stand up. It was like another Daisy had inhabited her.

'Daisy?' Tom asked hesitantly.

Putting her finger to his lips, she led him to the stairs. Climbing the stairs, it occurred to her she had discovered her own Ellodin, and her very own prince.

CHAPTER THIRTEEN

Blinking her eyes slowly, Daisy opened them, yawning as she did so. Stretching her legs and arms, she shuffled up the bed and checked the time. Snuggling back down, she revelled in how things had moved on from her first meeting with Tom. Remembering the tenderness as he had carried her to the sofa; the whisper of that kiss which became deeper and more energetic. Her complete abandonment of protocol as she led him to her fairy bower. There was no denying that she had become enchanted by Tom, experiencing sensations and desires new to her. No, it was more than that, they were alien to her. Having kept herself safe for so long, opening up her heart was tremendous.

It had been a couple of days since they had seen each other. When they finally came up for air, he had insisted on being a gentleman and returning home. It wouldn't have taken much for her to ask him to stay over, but it was early days. She knew that in a small place like Barley Ford, news would soon have spread if he'd left at breakfast. Daisy was still hesitant about complicating things.

Recalling how he had traced the shape of her body with his fingertips, she had struggled to concentrate on her explanation of needing to finalise her manuscript. Hushing her with his mouth, demanding and yet gentle, she had succumbed to the new desires stirring within her.

When they drew apart, Daisy had reluctantly expressed her wish for time to complete the last few chapters. She had been worried he would take it the wrong way, but the worry was soon dispelled as he held her close and kissed her long and hard before finally stepping out in to the cold night air.

Throwing the covers back, she left the warmth of her bed to

peer out of the curtains. A faint mist was dissipating from the fields and the world was gently waking up before her. Daisy knew she could not squander the time she had left in this most wonderful of places. Equally, she was on the home stretch of bringing her prince and princess together and expelling the enemies from the realm of Ellodin. Quickly washing and dressing, she ate a hasty breakfast and texted Sarah to check her arrival time. How had it got to Friday already? Another week had passed. She noticed another missed call from her dad. She knew she was delaying the inevitable by blotting out the flashes of memories. Fleetingly, she wondered if speaking to Ed again would help.

Staring at her laptop, and then at the gate where Bentley was standing like a sentinel, she grabbed a banana and headed out of the back door. Disregarding the urgency she felt to complete the last chapter, Daisy acknowledged that she partly wanted to focus on her own prince, rather than a make-believe one. But was she building her fantasy as a way to escape the reality of the conversation beckoning between herself and her dad?

After a few gentle words with Bentley, Daisy began striding across the dew-laden field. She was glad she had purchased her first pair of wellies. Breathing in the fresh, cool air, she felt alive, really alive for the first time in her life.

Reaching the brow of the hill, Daisy was still moved by the way the farm house rose out of the mist, greeting the morning. Announcing to the world it was still here and nothing would destroy it. Hesitantly, Daisy replayed her dad's last voicemail, asking again if he could visit. He was desperate to speak to her and she knew she was stalling. Even though she had begged for him to tell her what really happened, she had an inkling that this was why he wanted to see her and it made her feel uncomfortable. As she stood facing Tom's farm, she had to admit that perhaps Tom was an escape. What did she think was going to happen between them when it was time for her to leave? Was it better to face the reality that his life was here and hers was… well, where? Since arriving in Barley Ford, Daisy had felt such contentment. The situation with Tom was rapidly progressing. Trepidation settled around her, maybe she was just kidding herself after all. With a heavy heart, she turned and trudged back to her cottage. The last three-and-a-half weeks had been a revelation and she had accomplished far more than she thought she would. Greg had been reasonably happy with the last chapters she had sent to him so at least she was now back on track. It wasn't fair to lead Tom on when she had so much else in her life to sort out.

Reaching the gate, she pushed it open and was shocked to see her dad sitting on the garden bench.

'Dad, what are you doing here? This is a surprise.'

Watching as he stood up and walked towards her, Daisy felt the familiar tug tightening in her chest.

'Morning, good to see you too. You stopped answering my texts.'

'Sorry. It's good to see you.' She threw her arms around him and smelt his familiar lemon soap fragrance.

'You are a worry Daisy button. Though I have to say this country air must be agreeing with you. There is a glow about you.'

'I'm walking every day. This is such a beautiful place, you never did tell me how you knew about it.'

'Oh, you know me, I wouldn't be an award-winning travel journalist if I couldn't find a few off-the-grid places.'

'Well, it has certainly worked its restorative magic on me. Come on, I'll make us a drink.'

Once they had settled with drinks, and the pleasantries were over, Daisy sensed the mood change between them.

'You were right, Daisy, we need to talk and I figured it couldn't be put off any longer.' Dan Tremaine placed his mug on the table and rubbed his hands together.

'Can't it wait until I've finished the book? What is so pressing?'

A loud knock caused them both to swivel their heads in the direction of the door.

'Ah, seems you have a visitor.' Dan stood up.

Daisy saw it was Tom. Feeling the heat rise in her cheeks she raised her hand to try and rub the flush away.

'Tom, this is a surprise.'

Loitering in the doorway, Daisy noticed how his physicality filled the frame. A shot of embarrassment rushed through her as she recalled how their bodies had fitted together with such ease.

'I was passing. Sorry, I didn't realise you had a visitor.'

Stepping forward, Dan offered his hand to Tom.

'Hi, Dan Tremaine, Daisy's father.'

Awkwardly, Tom responded and shook the offered hand.

'Nice to meet you.' Tom drew his eyebrows together. 'I – it can wait till we catch up later.'

Daisy wished he would stay and save her from the conversation hanging in the air. Watching him fidget from one foot to another, she could see he was on edge.

'I've just made a pot of tea and you're welcome to join us.' She looked at him, willing him to say yes.

'Err, no, it's fine. I'll call you. Good to meet you Dan.'

'Likewise, please don't shoot off on my account.'

'No, it's fine, things to do. Nothing that can't wait.'

Daisy's heart lurched as she watched him march away, disappearing through the gate. Aware of her dad standing nearby, she shut the door.

'He didn't need to go. Seemed a pleasant enough chap, a bit nervy,' her dad said, settling himself back into his chair.

Daisy felt a tingle of nerves playing across her skin. There was something in Tom's manner which alarmed her. Was he regretting the other night and coming to call a halt to things? Rubbing the back of her neck, she attempted to shrug off the feeling of dread.

As she stood in the middle of the kitchen, irritation at her dad's arrival brewed inside her.

'I have work I need to do. Can't whatever brought you here wait?' Her voice snapped in the silence between them.

'No, it can't. I have a letter from your mum. She has asked me to give it to you, and hopes you will read it.' Slipping his hand inside his jacket, he pulled out a crumpled envelope and placed it on the table.

Staring at the envelope, Daisy's whole body tensed. The room swayed slightly and she grabbed hold of the counter top.

Rushing forward, Dan took hold of her and wrapped his arms around her.

'Talk to me Daisy, shout at me, anything but this.'

Collapsing into his chest, Daisy let out a long howl, the intensity of its pain searing the air. She could hardly breathe enclosed in her dad's arms. The years of blotting out the very heart of her anguish could be suppressed no longer. Sagging into her dad's body, she relinquished her fight and gave way to the shadows.

CHAPTER FOURTEEN

'I didn't expect to see you again so soon.' Edward held the door open as Daisy strode by him. Finding her way to his study, she sat down stiffly. It had been a long day and her head was pounding following her dad's visit.

'Me neither. Thanks for agreeing to see me at such short notice. Something unexpected has happened and I don't know what to do.'

'Ah, I see.'

Daisy watched as Ed crossed his legs. He had a kind face, though a hint of mischief glinted in his eyes. It was as if he was wearing a mask and if it slipped, he would be someone else. Perhaps it was the way his glasses were perched on the end of his nose, or his floppy jet black hair that suggested a casual side to his personality. Momentarily, she was curious about his life.

He coughed, interrupting her thoughts.

'Sorry, my dad has turned up. He's...' Daisy felt the words stick in her throat. 'My mum has written to me. I've spent most of the morning sobbing whilst Dad paced the room trying to make me feel better. I have spent my whole life holding my breath, waiting for the day when I would hear from her, when she finally came back. At the same time, I convinced myself a long time ago it would never happen. Just when I think I'm making headway, this comes out of the blue. He wouldn't tell me how she knew where to send it. He's holding something back Ed; I know he is. Why won't he just be honest with me?'

'I understand Daisy. We never want to willingly open ourselves to hurt. Perhaps this has been his way of keeping himself safe. Have you read the letter?'

'No!' Fishing in her pocket Daisy pulled out the envelope with the pinkish butterfly on the flap.

'What's stopping you?' Ed sat forward.

'There's this percolating fear spinning around inside me.' Daisy started rocking, still gripping the envelope. Her breath came in short gasps.

Leaning forward, Ed spoke in low gentle tone.

'Daisy, I need you to look at me.'

Daisy's fingers were fanned out across her chest. Raising her head, she looked at Ed.

'Okay, now listen to me, you need to focus on your breathing. Like we discussed before. One breath in and one long, slow breath out.

'That's it, nice and slow. In and out, one in and two out. There you go.'

Ed's soothing voice helped to calm her storm.

'When you're ready you can read it here, or we can talk.'

Her hands shaking, she opened the envelope and took out the letter inside.

Daisy unfolded the paper and began reading it aloud.

My dearest Daisy button,

Please don't stop reading this. Yes, it is from your mum and I cannot imagine what you are thinking, but I'm begging you to carry on.

I'm not sure how I can ever make amends for the anguish I have caused you and your dad.

Contrary to popular opinion, adults don't always make the best decisions for their children. I made a huge error.

I have watched you from afar over the years when I have been able to, and I have seen you grow into a beautiful young woman. Just like the butterfly I always knew you would become.

It was lovely to read you had included butterflies in the beginning of your story about Prince Oritane.

Daisy looked up from the letter and out of the window, tears streaming down her face.

'Almost two decades, and now she writes. Why? Here I go again, weeping like a mad woman.'

Ed fell back into his chair. Removing his glasses, he rubbed the bridge of his nose. It was several minutes before he spoke.

'I can only surmise that choices were made in the heat of the moment and the consequences were left to chance. Often there is no logic to decisions made in haste. Then we become cemented in them, afraid to change course.'

Daisy carried on reading quietly to herself.

I know you will be wondering why now, after all this time? I don't know how much your dad has attempted to explain things. I'm guessing he didn't and if he did, it didn't go too well.

Please, will you let me explain? It can be on your terms, wherever you wish, whenever you deem it right.

All I ask is the chance to tell my side of the story. Then you can decide what happens next.

I've included my phone and email details.
If you've reached this far in the letter, thank you my darling.
I have never stopped loving you.
Love Mum

Trembling, Daisy half crumpled the letter before re-straightening it and placing it back in the envelope.

'It's like hearing from a ghost. Dad still has his wall of silence. No explanation. Nothing. After all this time they are just words. She wants to explain her actions. On my terms. She said she never stopped loving me. Followed my career from afar. But she still stayed away.'

'You seem to have a palpable anger towards your dad. What's next? A conversation with him?'

'Yes, I need him to talk to me. What can be so awful that he just clams up? On the one hand all I ever wanted was for her to come home. On the other hand, I hated her for what she did. I buried myself away, trying to avoid both that pain and any future pain. Now I'm so confused. What does she think Dad might have tried to explain? Tell me what to do. What would you do?' Daisy pleaded.

'I am not you, Daisy. It is your decision to make. This is a big moment for you. The conflict I sense raging within you is perfectly natural.'

'Rage is a good word. You know, I think I have been running from this for so long that I don't know how to stand still with it.' Daisy twisted the letter in her hands.

'What does your heart tell you?'

Daisy lifted her head and tilted it to one side.

'My heart is bruised and battered.' Daisy's voice was barely a whisper. 'See her.'

'Then hold that close and reflect. Whatever path you choose, know it is your decision and own it. Speaking to your dad might be a starting point.'

Standing up, Daisy held her hand out to Ed.

'I'll never be able to thank you enough for being here to listen.'

Ed rose slowly from his chair and accepted her handshake.

Opening the door, Daisy hesitated before leaving.

'I hope you don't mind me calling you Ed? You don't match your name of Edward. You are too… Edward always makes me think of a stuffed shirt. You are nothing like that. Ed suits you. Tell me, do you enjoying being semi-retired?'

Ed's expression became serious before a slow smile spread across his face.

'I was always Edward to my mother. She hated anyone who shortened it. I haven't been called Ed for a number of years. I don't mind, I find it endearing. As for retirement, some days, I itch to be back in the fray. However, it was the right time for me to step back. I'm enjoying life now.' Ed began to laugh. 'I'm owning my decision.'

As Daisy walked down the path, she turned back to see Ed still standing in his doorway watching her. She was so glad to have met him. He was one of those people you met in life who earned a special place in your heart. He had helped her understand so much and she understood what he meant. Choice was almost the easy bit. It was the consequences you never considered.

Returning to her cottage, Daisy found a note from her dad,

explaining he had gone back to Lytton. More apologies, but he would call her in the evening.

Great Dad, that's really helpful. Who is running now?

Work was her only other therapy. Sarah would be here in a few hours and she'd done nothing today. Clicking her emails, she groaned when she saw several from Greg. He was keen to know how far away she was from the final copy.

'Not far now Greg, please be patient a little longer' she muttered to herself.

Clicking on *compose*, she took a deep breath and began typing.

'Dear Mum...', *nope, that's too familiar.* 'Mum', *okay, we'll start with that...*

Mum, receiving news about you was akin to having an electric shock.

You are right, you made the worst decision ever and I am still trying to process it all. Just for the record, Dad hasn't said anything. What is there for him to say? He just recites the same sentences, 'It was complicated', 'It was a long time ago'.

My main concern right now is to finish the final book of the Chronicles. You will just have to wait until I've done that.

Daisy.

Re-reading it, Daisy thought it sounded a bit pompous. She deleted it and wrote several more before deciding on her final version.

Mum, Well, as surprises go this was off the Richter scale. I wonder if you thought I would welcome you back with open arms? ~If so, you were wrong; right now, my arms are firmly shut. You are right about adults and decisions. By the way, Dad hasn't explained anything. He merely recites the same answers, 'It was complicated', 'It was a long time ago'.

I'm trying to finish Rose Water as I'm up against a deadline so you'll just have to wait a bit longer for any family reunion. No promises there will be one.

I'll be in touch. D.

Pressing send before she changed her mind, Daisy sat back and tried to imagine her mother receiving and reading it. Fleetingly, she thought of Granny Jenny and how devastated she must have been when Mum left. She still needed to tackle her dad about this explanation.

Daisy let out a long sigh. 'Enough delay, Princess Lilia, what is your next move?'

CHAPTER FIFTEEN

Daisy was busy making up a bed for Sarah when she heard a loud rapping on the front door. Glancing out of the front bedroom window, she saw a familiar bright blue Mini parked next to her own. Rushing down the stairs, she threw open the door and virtually fell into her best friend's arms.

'Oh, Sarah I'm so glad to see you. Come in, come in. I can't believe you made it.'

Laughing, Sarah stepped into the hall.

'Whoa, slow down. I'm amazed I made it here at all. How the hell did your dad find this place?'

'Beats me. Leave your bags there. Come on through, I'll put the kettle on. Oh Sarah, it's so good to see you. I have missed you.'

Throwing her arms around Sarah again, Daisy held on to her.

'Hey you. Is everything okay? Getting enough sleep?'

Sarah uncoiled herself from the hug, the glint in her eye not lost on Daisy.

Daisy jabbed Sarah's shoulder.

'No, it's nothing like that. I'm really happy you are here.'

Sometime later, after copious amounts of tea and biscuits, Daisy suggested they go for an amble round the village.

'Is that code for introducing me to the hunky farmer?' Sarah grinned.

'No, it is not. If you must know I haven't really seen him for a couple of days. He called this morning but didn't stay. Dad was here and I think it put him off.'

'You're not counting the days then?'

Daisy had no way to control the flush seeping across her cheeks.

'I've been preoccupied with the whole shambles that is my

family. Anyway, more of that later. Let's enjoy the last of the sunshine. The nights get quite chilly up here.'

Linking arms, the two girls wandered around the village. Daisy pointed out the pub, then Gerald's cottage.

'You were right, it is like it's from another era. Did your dad ever tell you how he came across this place? It would make a great backdrop to a story.' Sarah said, standing in front of the Celtic cross at the centre of the village green.

'You can imagine swirls of mist around this cross, then out steps the mad woman of Barley Ford.' Sarah burst out laughing.

'Honestly, you are the mad one. You are right though, it would be a great backdrop. I suppose I should be thinking of the next book. Greg tells me he has some news for me, but won't expand on what that news is.'

'Does that mean you have finished at last?' Sarah faced Daisy.

'Almost. I'm sorry, I was so looking forward to you visiting. It's just that Greg needs the rest of the chapters, like, yesterday. He's been battering my inbox with requests for the final copy for a few days. Come on, I need to show you the river. It's a brilliant place.'

Tucking her hands in her pockets, Daisy trooped off, Sarah following in her wake.

'Oh my goodness, it's beautiful Daisy. What a stunning place. It's so... I don't know, magical? You never said how your dad heard about it?' Sarah found a large boulder and sat down. Joining her, Daisy perched next to her friend.

'Apparently it's somewhere Mum mentioned to him. He said it was somewhere people she worked with came to recharge their batteries, whatever that means. This is my favourite part of the whole village. I love it here. At last, I can hear myself think. This has been my go-to place on my walks. Dorothy tells me that the original inhabitants of the village came down the river and settled on its banks before moving further inland.'

'You have to write about this place Daisy. There is so much magic here. It's uncanny, I don't think I have been anywhere quite like it.'

Sarah paused before carrying on, watching her friend.

'Daisy, I've known you a long time. I know when things aren't right. What's really wrong, you are pre-occupied and I know it isn't the book or farmer Tom.'

Picking up a stone, Daisy hurled it into the fast flowing water. Yanking the letter from her pocket, she handed it to Sarah.

'I don't mind you reading it.'

Sarah frowned and opened the letter. Daisy studied her face as she read it, hoping to see a clue to her thoughts. She was unprepared for the watery eyes.

'Oh my God Daisy, it's so sad. Yet it's so awful at the same time. What does she mean about your dad though? It's like he knows something he hasn't told you. What are you going to do?' Sarah slid her arm around Daisy's shoulders.

'I've emailed her. I had to do it whilst I was in the right mind. If I think about it too much I just get angry. I've seen Ed again. It helped to talk it through with him. The trouble is, I'm not sure I know how to forgive her. In my heart, I want to see her. Dad's been there for me through all the crap. It's hard to be as angry with him, whatever it is that he is hiding. Maybe that's why he scuttled off.'

Sitting together in silence as the sun dipped below the trees, the two women were oblivious to the figure on the bridge watching.

Something made Daisy look up towards the bridge, but there was no one there. Ghosts were hovering around her, the time was coming to lay them to rest.

CHAPTER SIXTEEN

Their weekend together unfolded in a lazy stretch of time. Having risen early, Daisy managed to complete the necessary work for Greg. She knew she had rushed it, but she just wanted to get it out of the way and spend time with her friend. She couldn't recall how long it had been since they had been together just as friends. Late into Saturday afternoon, a knock on the door disturbed their gossiping.

'Ooh! Might this be the elusive farmer, Tom?' teased Sarah.

'If it was, he would use the back door.' Daisy did find herself wondering what had happened to him, though. She'd mentioned Sarah visiting and maybe coming over for a drink. He hadn't answered any of her texts.

Opening the door, she revealed Dorothy. Her serious expression gave Daisy cause for concern.

'Dorothy, come in, my friend Sarah is here.'

Dorothy nodded and made her way to the front living room.

'Pleased to meet you,' Dorothy said quickly, then turned back to Daisy.

'Is everything okay Dorothy? Where's Harry?'

Sniffing, Dorothy perched on the edge of a chair.

'He's with Brian the vet. Came over a little peculiar whilst we were out earlier and he's not a young dog.'

Sarah sprang up from her chair, noticing immediately the elderly lady's distress.

'I think you need a shot of something. How about a quick snifter Dorothy?'

Dabbing her nose, she murmured that it was a kind offer.

'Does the vet have any idea what may be wrong?' Daisy asked gently.

'Oh, it's probably something he ate whilst we were out. He

has a habit of picking things up. They are often swallowed before I can retrieve them. He hates the vet. We've been together a long time, he and I. You never know. You think you are prepared, but then when it comes to it, dogs can't tell you what's wrong, you have to guess.'

'Here, I found this brandy at the back of the cupboard.' Sarah placed the glass on a table next to Dorothy.

'That's not the reason why I called round, though I appreciate your thoughtfulness. I've seen you wandering around the village giggling like schoolgirls. It's so refreshing to see a bit of life in the old place.'

Daisy laughed, 'We are terrible when we get together. We were always getting separated at school for chattering.'

'I can imagine. Good to have some company. My reason for calling is that I wondered if you had seen Tom lately? He was due to call in and try to sort out my chimney. It's been blowing smoke back into the room. It's not like him to not call in.'

Feeling slightly embarrassed that Dorothy thought she may know where he was, Daisy blushed.

'Er, no, I haven't seen him for a couple of days. Sarah and I were going to take a walk over there later. If he's in, I'll remind him about the chimney.'

'Thank you my dear, that's sweet of you. Well, I must go, the vet may be trying to call. Appreciate the booster.' Dorothy raised her glass.

'If you need anything Dorothy, please don't hesitate to knock and let us know how Harry is.'

'I will. Thank you.'

Reaching the brow of the hill, Daisy leaned across and stopped Sarah in her tracks.

'What is it? Have you spotted him?' Sarah started bouncing around.

'For goodness' sake Sarah, you're obsessed. You binge-watch too many romantic boxsets. No, I want you to look at the view.'

Screwing up her face, Sarah took a moment to soak in the

surroundings. She let out a long whistle.

'This is something else. You'll hate me saying this, but it reminds me of a Jane Austen novel. Any minute now, farmer Tom will coming striding up the hill and call, "Daisy, my Daisy, where have you been all my life."' Sarah burst into fits of giggles.

Daisy rolled her eyes and pushed her away playfully.

'Will you behave. I agree, it is very Austen. However, Tom is nothing like an Austen character. He lacks the refinement. More a lumberjack type. Though he does have a sensitive side. Have you ever considered writing a romantic romp? I reckon it would be a sell out.'

'Can you blame me Daisy? Neither of us have had much success in the love stakes. Since Steve, I haven't been out with anyone that I'd consider a second date with.'

'I still can't believe you two were together for more than a year, then he just announces he's got a new job and is off to the other side of the world. Scumbag.'

'When he first mentioned it, I was certain he was going to ask me to go with him. Misjudged that. Hey ho. But you are no better, all wrapped up in your world of Ellodin. Look at us, what a sad pair we make. I guess the prospect of anything remotely romantic is exciting. Even if I'm feeding off your romantic adventure.'

'Romantic adventure? Do you think that's all he is? An adventure? I've been thinking about him a lot and I don't know whether I'm distracting myself again. Ed reckons it's a default mechanism to stop me facing my own reality. Anyway, since Tom and I spent the night together, I've hardly seen him. He hasn't answered any of my messages. Not a good sign. I've probably put him off. Messed-up author with family issues. I took a chance Sarah and I think it has back fired. Now I just feel stupid.'

Sarah walked over and put her arm around Daisy.

'You don't know why he hasn't been in touch. Didn't you say he called when your dad was visiting? Maybe he got scared away. Anyway, more fool him. We all have to take that chance

Daisy. I don't know whether it's an adventure or not. I do know you deserve to give yourself a break. Come on, let's go down there and be farmer groupies. Imagine his face when the two of us turn up.'

Virtually skipping down the hill, they arrived quite breathless at the back door. Knocking loudly, Daisy found it odd that no one answered. Deciding to try the front door, she met Mrs B pushing her bicycle down the path.

'Afternoon Daisy.'

'Hello Mrs B. This is my friend Sarah. We've just popped over to see Tom.'

Mrs B pushed on past, speaking as she went.

Daisy and Sarah followed behind her.

'Is everything okay Mrs B?'

Mrs B stopped suddenly, causing Daisy to nearly run into her.

'You'd best come in and I'll make us some tea.'

Anxiously, the two friends followed her into the kitchen. A weight plummeted in Daisy's stomach. There was no sign of life in the kitchen.

Mrs B poured tea from the large brown teapot and passed a plate of chocolate biscuits to her.

'Tom has gone to Scotland.'

'Scotland?'

'Yes, there was some trouble with his sister. I'm only here today because the holiday cottages are due visitors and I need to sort them out.'

'Trouble? Is she okay?'

'Tabby is a handful at the best of times. Highly strung and always dramatic. Caused her mother a great deal of worry as she was growing up. Didn't help that their father was away so much. Still, families… you can't choose them, can you? Don't you worry Daisy, she'll be right. She's not ill if that's what you are thinking.'

'She seemed so composed when I was here. Even though her tone was a bit sharp.'

Putting her cup down, Mrs B stared at its contents.

'She always likes to be queen bee and command the room. We all know what she's like and we ignore it. Hard to know that, if you've just met her. But don't you fret about her.'

Gradually, as Daisy dipped her biscuit in her tea, something dawned on her.

'I never got chance to properly thank you for your red tin the other day. Life has not been easy of late.'

'Red tin? Sounds intriguing,' Sarah added, munching a biscuit.

'Apparently, whenever there's an emergency, a red tin full of gooey cakes is brought out. It certainly helped me.'

'Life's never a straight road. You seem very young to have the need to come to Barley Ford, if you don't mind me saying?' interjected Mrs B.

'I'm a writer, I came here to finish a book I'm working on. I've been under a lot of pressure lately and my dad had heard of this place. He suggested it would serve as a retreat for me. It's certainly a one-off. Nothing like I was expecting. Oh, by the way, Dorothy was expecting Tom to clean her chimney. She said it's unusual for him to not let her know if he's not around.'

A stillness rested in the kitchen.

Mrs B stood up suddenly and started to clear things away. Daisy had the impression they were being dismissed.

'If Tom calls, I'll let him know you've been. Can you tell Dorothy where he is?' Mrs B carried on clearing the table.

'We will.' Reluctantly Daisy lifted herself from the chair.

'You know, Tom has been a lot brighter since you arrived.'

Daisy stood still, slightly taken aback. 'Was he miserable then?'

'The path he walks is not always easy. It's been good to see him smile a bit more. Mind how you go. Don't mean to be rude but I do need to get on. Nice to meet you, Sarah.'

Daisy and Sarah meandered back to the cottage much more quietly.

'Funny, what she said back there don't you think?' queried Sarah as they reached the gate to the garden.

'What do you mean?'

'That Tom is brighter. He has a difficult path. Just an odd thing to say, particularly as you haven't known him that long. Maybe she's sizing you up as a lady of the manor? It's all very mysterious. Crumbs Daisy, there's so much going on beneath the surface here, it's a writer's paradise.'

Daisy glanced back to the brow of the hill. What family troubles was he having to deal with? Was it really any of her business? Perhaps it was just a fling to keep her from facing up to her own issues.

'What?' Daisy realised Sarah had spoken to her. 'I suppose it is when you think about it. Funny, I've not clicked to any of that. I've been so intent on finishing the Chronicles that I've missed what's been there in front of me. You are right though, there's something very compelling about this place.'

'Well, I guess that's sorted out the next book then?'

'Come on, let's take a bottle round to Dorothy's and see how Harry is. Your final night doesn't need be wasted on absent men.'

Biting her lip, Daisy gripped the back door key in her hand and resolved to put Tom firmly to the back of her mind so she could enjoy Sarah's last night.

CHAPTER SEVENTEEN

After the frivolity and fun of the weekend she'd spent with Sarah, Monday morning seemed flat and featureless.

Chewing her pen, Daisy lamented how there had been no sign of Tom, but she didn't want to bother Mrs B again. When she had explained to Dorothy that Tom was visiting his parents, Dorothy had seemed unsurprised. Sarah had thought Dorothy was being very tight-lipped about the whole situation with Tabby.

It had been wonderful having Sarah to stay. They had even managed to bring Alex's blog up-to-date and answer some of the comments readers had left. One in particular had explained how reading the Chronicles had got her through a difficult time. The books had been so absorbing that they had taken her away from her own problems. Daisy had also enjoyed just chit-chatting about general everyday things. It had been so long since she had talked about anything other than her writing. There was a time she and Sarah would meet regularly, just to catch up.

Even more surprisingly, there had been some messages of support from the women's group she had spoken at, all hoping she would return and share some writing secrets. Sarah had asked if there were any trade secrets, but in truth there were not. Just damn hard work and determination not to give up at the first hurdle. Daisy was quick to point out that she had been lucky.

Sarah was right about one thing, she needed to get to the end of what now felt like a marathon. That had been the whole point of coming to Barley Ford. Sighing, Daisy noticed her email icon blinking.

'Please be kind, Greg,' she said out loud.

By the time she had read the message, her mood had lifted slightly. He was very happy with what she had sent and he was clear that the deadline was achievable. He went on to tell her about all the interest and various interviews he was beginning to line up for her. The circus was not far away, then.

'Yeah, well, I have a huge barrier in the way and the prince is being very stubborn regarding the princess.' It had not escaped her notice that their relationship had been a slow burn where as she and Tom had propelled at a rate of knots. It had been so out-of-character for Daisy to sleep with him. Yet it had seemed so natural. She knew some guys moved on after that, but Tom hadn't seemed liked that. However, she'd not always been a great judge of character.

Breaking the mood, her phone buzzed and her heart sank when she saw it was her dad.

'Hi Dad.'

'Daisy, how you are doing?'

'How come you left so suddenly?'

Daisy picked up on the pause.

'Dad?'

'Figured you might need some space to digest the letter.'

'Yes. Like, what does Mum mean about you explaining something to me?'

'Do we have to get into that now? I just called to make sure you were okay.'

'We need to get into it at some point Dad. Isn't it about time you were straight with me?'

'Is there any chance I could come over?'

A frisson of resentment swelled within her.

'No Dad, not unless you are ready to talk. And I mean talk.'

Daisy sucked in her breath.

'I need to knuckle down. Greg is badgering me constantly and I have corrections to do. I have no more excuses left.'

The silence down the phone spoke volumes and Daisy felt sick. In all their years together, she had never spoken to him in such a tone.

'I understand. How about I call you nearer the end of the week, to see how you are getting on?'

'That would be great. Who knows, by then I may be finished.'

Her finger hovered over the cancel button. 'Dad, I do love you.'

'I love you too, Daisy button.'

The line went dead and the sickness lingered. Pushing the laptop away, Daisy slumped against the back of her chair. Suddenly everything was starting to pile in again. Her flow was receding. When she had sent the final chapters to Greg, he had emailed back to say he liked the ending but had expected it to be punchier. He was pleased she was almost at the end and could she look at his editorial notes. Throwing down her pen, she stood up, slamming her laptop shut. She decided to go and see Dorothy. Daisy found her a very grounded woman and with Harry home and recovering, it gave her the perfect excuse to visit.

'Daisy, how lovely to see you. I've just made tea. Gerald is here checking up on the patient. Please come in.'

Dorothy bustled about as Daisy walked into the living room. She was taken aback to see Ed. This could be embarrassing.

'Gosh, a houseful. I didn't mean to intrude.' Daisy was uncertain what to do and as if sensing her disquiet, Ed stood up.

'No need to worry Daisy, I was just on my way out.'

Ed stared at her and his eyebrow arched, as if he wanted to know she was doing alright. She gave a weak smile.

'Please don't go on my account. I'm looking for an excuse to delay working.'

'You play hooky for a cuppa and then back to it, eh? That ending won't write itself.'

'I don't think I have ever drunk so much tea and eaten so much cake since I arrived here.'

Ed grinned as he left the room. By now Harry was in full yapping mode, breaching all protocols and putting everyone at ease.

'Well, Harry looks as if he's on the mend.' Daisy laughed as she bent down to stroke him.

Dorothy entered the room tutting at her pet and Gerald muttered something about hairy mutts and Daisy laughed at the scene. Sitting down, her mood brightened, especially when the fruit cake appeared. It seemed that life in this village revolved around cake.

'He's like a cat with nine lives that one.' Dorothy tutted, cutting a slice of cake.

'I'm glad he's better. What was the problem?' asked Daisy, balancing her plate away from Harry.

'Digestion issue, let's leave it at that. Your friend gone?' asked Dorothy.

'Yes, it was great to see her. It's been ages since we had a girlie weekend. I hadn't realised how much I missed her company. I always seem to be attached to my laptop,' Daisy sighed.

'Dorothy tells me you are a writer Daisy. Plenty of stories around here if you ever get stuck for ideas.' Gerald spoke gruffly.

'Now, now, Gerald, the girl has enough on her plate without you filling her head with gossip. Take no notice Daisy.'

'Sarah said exactly the same thing. There is an aura about this place. When I've finished the Chronicles, I shall come back and scout the next book,' Daisy laughed. Gerald tutted once more and nodded.

'No news of Tom then?' Dorothy asked, suddenly looking directly at Daisy.

Daisy shook her head. Dorothy obviously reckoned they were in constant communication. Truth was she had not heard a thing from him. She realised how much she missed him.

'I imagine that sister of his is keeping him busy. Always was a flighty piece,' Gerald offered as he lifted his teacup.

'Gerald is never one to mince his words. You have plenty to say this morning. Whatever will our young visitor be thinking? Families have their own business to sort out and it's nothing to do with us,' Dorothy scolded.

Daisy detected a distinct cooling of the atmosphere and wondered what Gerald could have meant.

'She did seem a bit curt when I met her the other week. She was leaving to visit her parents then. Tom appeared annoyed that she was going and leaving him to sort out the holiday cottages. What does she do for a job?' Daisy asked tentatively.

There was a brief exchange of looks between Gerald and Dorothy. Daisy would have loved to know what wasn't being said.

'Oh yes, she does work but it involves a lot of travel. Causes a bit of a grumble because the farm is shared between her and Tom. He gets a bit niggled that she's absent so much,' Dorothy informed her.

'My mum travelled with her job. It caused a bit of friction and then she left us completely. Although it was hard, at least we all knew where we stood.' Daisy stopped herself, realising how sharp she sounded.

'Parents are always trying to juggle their lives. We don't think our parents have lives, that they are just Mum and Dad,' Dorothy mused.

'Must have been hard for you Daisy, girls need their mothers,' offered Gerald.

'I managed. Dad was great, he gave up a lot.'

'No contact with her then, your mother?' Gerald sat up slightly.

'Er no, she just up and went. I do know she worked with the military. She was some sort of profiler. Dad has never been very forthcoming about what happened. You get used to things after a while.'

'You must forgive Gerald, Daisy. He likes a bit of intrigue,' Dorothy interjected.

'No worries, I'm just not used to talking about it really. Anyway, I think I've lingered long enough. My laptop calls.' Daisy stood up.

'Anytime my dear, you are more than welcome.'

Dorothy walked Daisy to the front door. Placing her hand on Daisy's arm, Dorothy spoke quietly.

'Don't be too hard on your mother Daisy. She must have had her reasons. Mothers don't leave their children readily.'

Daisy tilted her head to one side and was about to speak when the phone rang on the hall table.

'Ah, better answer that. Take care my dear.'

Walking back to her cottage, Daisy was baffled. It was strange, she thought, that Dorothy had voiced the same opinion as Ed about mothers. Then there was Gerald's comment about girls needing their mothers.

Barley Ford was the most alluring place she had ever visited. For many reasons, it was going to be hard to leave when the time came.

CHAPTER EIGHTEEN

It was late into the evening when Daisy finally locked the doors, closed the curtains and wearily climbed the curved stairs to bed, musing to herself that it was like climbing the stairs in a fairy house as they twisted around before finally reaching the top.

As she lay in the darkness, save the glimmer from the moon peeking through the gap in the curtains, Daisy pressed play in her head and watched the scenes of the previous days and weeks play back.

The uncertainty of leaving everything familiar behind her had paid off. She conceded that her dad deserved credit for suggesting Barley Ford. She began to feel curious about the link between her mum and this place. Is this where she slinked off to after the chaos she left behind, claiming her own sanctuary? At least the panic attacks had lessened and even though the ending of the Chronicles was still elusive, she had made headway, much to the delight of Greg. What about her dad? He had yet to tell her of this mysterious explanation. Did he know more about her mother's sudden departure than he had told her? If so, why had he kept it to himself all these years? Rolling onto her side, Daisy's hand stroked the empty pillow next to her. An ache caught in her throat. Having acted out of character and given herself over to living in the moment, Tom had now removed himself and become incommunicado. She couldn't work out if she was disappointed in herself or if she genuinely missed his company. She had been so convinced there was a spark between them. The night they spent together was delicious and letting out a long, lonesome sigh she doubted she would ever feel that way again. Perhaps Tom was so wrapped up in his family saga that he had no time to think about her. It sounded like his sister was a handful. Maybe she was being unfair. After all, what did she know about the family, other than the few things they had shared with her? Though Dorothy and Gerald seemed united in thinking that Tabitha was a bit of a flighty bird... perhaps she was one of those people who fled when things got tough. Daisy suddenly wondered if her mother had fled for that very reason.

Dorothy and Gerald were very sweet. Daisy wondered if they had once been an item. There was a comforting familiarity between them that could only come from knowing each other so well. Daisy found that she had become very fond of Dorothy, and thinking of Dorothy brought Granny Jenny to mind. It had been so long since she had last spoken to her and even longer since they had last spent time together. When she finally got her head straight, she needed to rectify that.

However things panned out between her and Tom, she owed him a debt of gratitude for fixing her up with Ed. Speaking to him had been weird to begin with, but he was so unflustered by everything she had spoken about. He had helped quell her rising anxiety and taught her how to manage it. It was early days, but she was getting better at using the techniques. There was still the issue of how she was going to handle her mum. Daisy had a growing sense of intrigue about her, and part of her wanted to see her and get to the bottom of why she left. Another part of her, which Ed had explained was her inner child, was still angry.

Daisy was soothed by the silence. The odd squawk of a pheasant, the call of an owl. It was as if Barley Ford hovered between two worlds.

'Oh my God, just like Ellodin,' she called out to the empty space around her. She sat up suddenly, clicking the bedside lamp on. Reaching for her notebook, she began frantically scribbling notes.

Everyone had expected the prince and princess to come together and meld their two kingdoms. A surge of energy fizzed through Daisy, and a lightbulb flashed on in her head. At last she knew now how their story needed to end.

Daisy worked late into the night before she was satisfied with her new ending. Exhausted, she fell asleep, pen in hand.

Waking in a fog, she momentarily struggled to establish her surroundings. Strewn across the duvet were her notes and crumpled pieces of paper. Gathering them up, she clambered out of bed.

Pulling back the curtains, she welcomed the new day. During her hours of writing, she realised that she had hardly thought about Alex in the last few weeks. Even when she was answering some of the queries on her website, she had not even given a thought to being Alex. In her book, that was real progress. Daisy knew she still had not taken back full control of her life. She had almost sleepwalked into a world not of her conscious making. She had also come to understand how much of her own story she had woven through the tale of the prince and princess. She had been acting out in words her own losses and battles.

Daisy could see Bentley standing patiently by her fence. An idea formulated in her exhausted brain and she decided to act before it faded away.

After breakfast, Daisy made her first call of the day.

'Daisy, it's great to hear from you. How are you doing?' Greg's relief was evident in his tone.

'It's done Greg. I'm emailing it over as we speak. Be prepared though, I've changed a few things and it's altered where the story ends. Let me know as soon as you've read it.' Pressing send as she talked, Daisy sent a little prayer with it.

'Changed? How much change? Should I be worried?'

'No, you should be glad and happy and sighing with relief. I've delivered. Look, just read it and then let me know what you think. I have some errands to run so don't panic if you can't get hold of me.'

'Actually, Daisy, there is something I need to run by you. I was going to wait, but what the hell. There's a movie deal in the offing for the whole trilogy. We need to have a serious talk.'

Daisy almost fell into the chair, dropping the phone as she did.

'Hello? Daisy, are you there?'

Breathe Daisy, just breathe. You've got this. Picking up her phone, she accidentally cut Greg off.

Daisy took a moment to drink in what Greg had just announced. A movie? She never saw that coming. Never in a million years had she ever thought about a film.

Her phone buzzed, she answered.

'Greg, sorry, I dropped the phone. I'm stunned. I don't know what to say. I was never expecting anything like that.'

'Me neither, but it happens. One of your biggest fans is a director. Look, one thing at a time. I'll read the new draft and get back to you. It is so fantastic. Great news, isn't it?'

Laughing and feeling giddy, Daisy agreed.

She needed to share her news, but couldn't get hold of anyone. Typical, just when she wanted to speak to people. Leaving messages for her dad and Sarah felt like a bit of an anti-climax.

Glancing out of the window, she was shocked to see Tom at the gate. Daisy ran to the door and flung it open. Her heart in her mouth, she raced to meet the figure now waving to her.

Daisy had a flash of an image at the end of a movie where the hero and heroine finally get together. In her heart she knew she was a long way from that. Tom represented something pure and honest. He had little regard for the world she inhabited, only the daily routine of keeping his animals and his family safe and well.

Gathering her up in his arms, Daisy found herself being swung around.

'Daisy, Daisy, well, I wasn't expecting this. Looks like you've missed me.'

Tom brushed her hair away from her face, his hand grazing her cheek.

Daisy wondered if the glow she was experiencing could be seen from space.

'I've missed you too,' whispered Tom, his hold strengthening around her.

Without wavering, their lips anchored to each other. With Tom pressing himself against her, Daisy allowed the moment to consume her and all thoughts of anything else were washed away as the kiss strengthened.

Gradually, the fever of the moment slowed and Tom pulled away first. 'Now, that was a welcome worth having. I could only ever dream that you shared my feelings.'

Leaning into him, Daisy was aware of a fluttering in her stomach. She had never imagined that anyone could really feel like this. Without warning, an image of her mum and dad embracing in the kitchen at home flashed into her head. Laughter ringing in her ears. *This must have been what it was it was like for my parents,* she thought. Her dad had always told her that her mum was The One, and up until now, Daisy had never really understood. Whatever was happening between her and Tom, she had to admit it was more than just a romantic encounter.

'Who could dream that one kiss could cause such a reaction?'

Daisy stepped back and looked up at Tom. Her heart was racing so fast, she barely had time to answer before Tom lowered his head and kissed her, properly this time. Daisy's whole body melted into his. If she was dreaming, she never wanted it to end. Soon enough, she would be jarred awake by reality. For now, she would luxuriate in the mesh of heat binding them in this moment.

Finally, breaking the spell, Tom lifted his head away, delicately tracing the shape of Daisy's face with his finger.

'I certainly wasn't expecting any of this, Daisy Tremaine. You are bewitching.'

Daisy grinned, every inch of her sparkling like a thousand glimmering lights.

'Life is full of surprises. Your timing is impeccable, I've literally just got off the phone with Greg. He told me some hot shot director is interested in making the Chronicles into a film. Imagine that. Then wham, out of the blue, there you were.'

Laughter burst from them both.

'Sounds to me like you have been offered an amazing opportunity, Daisy.'

Daisy acknowledged with a half-hearted nod. She couldn't help noticing his shoulders sag slightly.

'I have. I've been lucky and achieved everything most writers strive for in a lifetime. But that's the dilemma. I've never really had any time to be me, Daisy Tremaine. Until I met you. Then suddenly, I didn't need to be anyone except myself. You asked nothing of me. Over the years, since Mum left, I turned into this writing machine. It was always an excuse to stay in my room and hide. Thanks to you introducing me to Ed, my perception of many things has changed. I don't need to hide anymore. You've been part of that process and have helped me see how things could be different. I never expected to come here and meet someone who makes me feel the way you do.'

'It's been a surprise to me too Daisy. That's the reason I needed to let you know I was back. Mrs B told me you had been over. I arrived home late last night. I should have told you I was going away, but everything happened so quickly. Plus the reception is rubbish where my folks live. Forgive me?'

Daisy sighed, how could she not forgive him?

'Any chance we can meet later? How about I cook this time, give us chance to talk?' Tom's smile reached his twinkling eyes.

'Talk?' Daisy smirked and put her hand to his cheek.

'I'd love that, thank you.'

Kissing Daisy full on her lips, she responded naturally.

'I need to go before I lose control.'

'Then go, I'll see you later.' Beaming with happiness, Daisy watched him stride away across the field, thinking her heart would burst. A different kind of bursting to all the stuff that had consumed her when she first spoke to Ed. It dawned on Daisy that she had not asked Tom about his sister. Maybe that would be part of the chat later. It was turning out to be quite a day. Plus she had completely forgotten that she was going to walk over and ask to ride Bentley. Oh well, maybe another time.

CHAPTER NINETEEN

'I guess my cooking's not as good as I hoped,' Tom ventured as he poured himself another beer.

'Oh no, it was delicious.' Daisy laid her knife and fork on her plate.

'Nope! I'm not convinced, look at all the pie you have left. I never took you for someone who worried about what they ate.'

'What? So, you think I'm a bit on the chubby side, then?'

Tom put his beer down, leaned forward and smiled.

'On the contrary, your curves send me wild. It's just that you strike me as the kind of woman who doesn't go in for all that, "Ooh I can't eat that" etc. Believe me, I've known girls like that. Drives me mad.'

'Ah, so there has been a bevy of beauties then?'

A raucous laugh burst out of Tom.

'Oh yeah, lining them up at the farm gate. Being stuck out here kind of makes that tricky. I have discovered that people have a funny idea of what farming is all about. For instance, take the lambing season. All those adorable little lambs. There was a girl, quite some time ago now, she was horrified when I told her they would be on someone's plate in a few months. Needless to say, she left pretty smartish after that.'

A serious expression veiled Tom's face.

'It's a hard life. There's hardly any money in farming these days, hence the reason the holiday cottages were a great idea. It was part of the reason my dad moved away. He couldn't stomach it anymore, the strain of making ends meet became too much. Not that he isn't comfortably off, but he knew to keep this place going, it needed to be able provide a solid income. I think he ran out of energy for it all.'

Daisy listened attentively as he spoke, glad of the diversion of someone else's life.

'Was he ill?'

'Not exactly. Tired, I guess. Even after he allegedly retired, he often went to London doing consultancy work. It exhausted him in the end. Initially, it was Mum who suggested a sabbatical to Scotland. Far enough away that they could recharge and not get dragged into things here. It gave him time to work out if retirement was really for him. I think he resisted it at first. When he finally agreed that it was time to step back properly, he decided I could stay and give it a go with my "new-fangled" ideas.' Tom did inverted commas in the air. 'Mum didn't count on Dad liking being the laird so much and he decided they should stay up there. Hard for Mum, she loved it here. Dad explained the farm could be signed over to me, otherwise they would sell. I couldn't bear it, nor could my sister. In spite of her dramatics, she is as passionate about this place as I am.'

Tom pushed his food around his plate.

'That's when your sister came up with the cottage idea?'

'Yes, genius really, even though she's never really made this her life. Once you are connected with the land that's it. It's there for life. Well, that's the romantic notion anyway.'

'But wasn't your dad connected?'

'You know, I never really asked him. I suppose he was to begin with. Like I said, he worked in London for years and when he inherited the farm, he attempted to spend more time here. He did have a brother, but he died quite young, so I think it fell to Dad whether he wanted it or not.'

'He could have sold it.'

'Yes, true, but he had to try. He did confess to me that being the one to let it go was a greater burden than actually trying to make a go of it. I think in the beginning they enjoyed the peace here; but it doesn't suit everyone. Barley Ford is very remote and made up of a hotchpotch of folks. Some from the city, escaping the rat race, and those who have lived here all their lives, like Mrs B. Funny thing is, I couldn't imagine living anywhere else. Tabby acts like she is a prisoner to the ancestral home, but underneath it she is as devoted as I am.'

He sat back drinking his beer. It felt to Daisy as if he was staking out his position between them. He belonged here. Embedded in the foundations of the family home. She wondered what that meant for the future of the relationship. Was there even a future? The jury was still out on that.

'There is a wilderness about the place, yet it is so tranquil. I can imagine how bleak it must be in winter. I never expected the effect it has had on me. At last, I can hear myself think. I know it sounds dramatic, but I think it has helped me grow into myself, Daisy. Giving me the time to think and reflect. To finish the Chronicles.' She paused, *maybe even find love, someone to trust at last*, she thought. Gosh! Was that it? Was she in love with him?

'How are those reflections going? Time to move on, or take a chance?'

Daisy averted her eyes and poked the pie around the plate. What did he mean, take a chance?

'I'm not sure, there's still the complication with my mum.' Daisy bit her lip. 'That day you came over and Dad was there, he'd brought me a letter from her. How bizarre is that?'

Tom immediately sat up, resting his elbows on the table.

'Must have been quite a shock. Has it made that situation any clearer for you? I could never imagine my life without my mum?'

'No not really.' Daisy sat looking at the man opposite. He was a complete contrast to blond-haired, blue-eyed Prince Oritane. Tom's skin was weathered, his cheeks reddened by being outdoors so much. You could be forgiven for thinking he dyed his hair as the copper sheen glistened under the lights. Daisy was conscious their two worlds were colliding.

'Come on you, time for the fireside.' With one movement, he had lifted her out of her chair and carried her through to the room next door to the kitchen.

'This is getting a habit Tom Weaver, you carrying me around the place. I could get used to it.' Daisy laughed, allowing herself to be swept along on the tide of anticipation.

Tom carefully laid her on the large sofa near the roaring fire.

'I'll be back.'

Daisy stared at the flames licking the back of the chimney. She had been completely swept away by his behaviour. In her wildest imaginings, she never pictured herself in this scenario. If someone told her this was to be her home for the rest of her life, she would be quite content to remain in this magical place that had purged her of so many ghosts. Was she getting carried away with her own fantasy? The collision of the world she created in her story and the happy ending she desired so much in her own?

She knew her dad would take her mum back into his life in a heartbeat. He had never stopped loving or missing her. What kind of love was that? She was astonished it even existed. The endurance of those feelings and the need to still be with her. It was a love many couldn't comprehend. Yet a small part of her now conceded she was beginning to understand.

Breaking through her meanderings, Tom reappeared carrying a tray with two cut glass brandy goblets and two bright red dishes.

'Brandy and ice cream, it's the best cure for shock. Ice cream first, as the cold reawakens our bodies. Then the brandy, warming us ready for relaxation.'

The glimmer in his eyes was not lost on Daisy. As he plonked himself next to her, she couldn't help grinning. She wanted to remain forever in this moment.

Accepting the bowl of ice cream, she savoured each spoonful.

'Am I in shock then? Mmm, I love honeycomb ice cream,' she said, licking her lips.

'It's me who is in shock, Daisy. From that first morning you stood on the doorstep shivering, when I first delivered the logs, to now. It's too fantastic to have even dreamed about. Yet I have on occasions dreamt that one day the right girl would come along,' Tom admitted.

Sitting up straighter, Daisy stopped eating. The energy in the room shifted and she felt a slight shiver run through her. The right girl? Was she that girl? Afraid to acknowledge his words, she changed the subject.

'Tom, when I came over the other day, Mrs B didn't seem surprised you had dashed off to Scotland. Is Tabby okay?'

Twisting round, he looked up at Daisy.

'Mrs B has been with the family forever. Mum met her at some village do. They became friends and when she realised that Mum could do with some help, she offered her services. In the beginning it was just odd things like the ironing and maybe some light cleaning. There was always a steady stream of visitors. Like I said before, they hosted people from London, colleagues of Dad's I think mostly. We were always bustled off to bed. Mrs B became firmly established as a housekeeper, but not living in. Mum sings her praises as if she is a saint.'

'She seemed insistent that your place was here.'

'That sounds like Mrs B.' Tom carried on eating.

'If you don't want to talk about your sister, I understand.'

Swapping his dish for his brandy, Tom warmed the goblet in his hands before taking a drink.

'It's not that I don't want to tell you Daisy, it's just with everything you have going on, I figured you didn't need my family woes as well. Ready for your brandy?'

Daisy nodded.

'Why do I get the impression this is something you do from time to time?'

'You'd be right, it was my sister who started it. She was about thirteen I think, lumbered with looking after her baby brother. Mum and Dad were on a rare night out. We had ice cream, even though it was freezing and blowing a gale outside. Then Tabby thought it would be great fun to try the brandy afterwards. Consequently, we were both horrendously sick in the middle of the night and had to confess to Mum what we'd done.'

'Oh no, what did she say?'

'What any mother would say; don't tell your father.'

They laughed quietly together, relaxed in one another's company.

'About your parents, it must be so confusing for you?' Tom asked.

'It's so mixed up. On the one hand, I'm mad as hell. On the other hand, my curiosity has grown. I think anger has given way to just wanting to know why.'

'Could you live with yourself if you turned her away?'

'No, I couldn't. I have missed her so much, it hurts. Ed has encouraged me to listen to them both. There's a piece of the jigsaw missing and I can't get my head round it.'

Tom put his glass down and took Daisy's from her. Pulling her to him, he circled his arms around her and held her close.

'Someone once told me that forgiveness was the greatest gift you give anyone. If you were the parent that's what you would do isn't it? Forgive and try to move on.'

Snuggled in against Tom's chest, the softness of his shirt soothed Daisy's cheek. Inhaling the fragrance of sandalwood, she murmured a quiet 'yes'.

'So that's the answer then, Daisy, you don't need to beat yourself up. Just forgive and allow yourself to move on and start a new chapter in your life.'

Lifting her face to his, he kissed her lips delicately.

'My sister has caused us some concerns over the years. My mum and dad just take her in, cosset her, make sure she is fine and then send her on her way again. Mum says that the life she has chosen makes it hard to do anything else.'

'What is her life?'

'Ah now that,' Tom kissed her forehead, 'is a story,' he kissed her cheek, 'for another day.' He kissed her other cheek.

'We have our own story and it starts right now.'

Kissing her earnestly this time, Daisy could swear her toes turned upwards as the warmth of the brandy and the desire to rip Tom's shirt off fused together. Whatever the future held, why shouldn't she, just this once, look out for herself.

CHAPTER TWENTY

One of the greatest surprises to Daisy during her few days without writing was how much she slept, ate and lolled around in the garden. She became amused by the antics of the sparrows as they fluttered from the hedge to the grass to the bird table and back to the hedge. It was like a choreographed ballet. Writing for children had never entered her head before, but a sprig of an idea was taking root. She had taken a number of photos of the different birds which flew backwards and forwards and shared them on her blog. She'd been amazed by the response from some of her followers. She was keen to keep a lid on Barley Ford and was careful not to mention where she had taken the photos as she didn't want to be the one to spoil it. Daisy grimaced and shook her head at the image of the Celtic cross at the centre of the green being a hotspot for fans. There was no way she wished to contribute to wreaking havoc on this serene enclave.

Hearing a car engine outside, she popped her head up to look out of the window. Recognising the car, she groaned. It was her dad. Sluggishly, she dragged herself to the door.

Standing behind it, she waited for the knock. Her heart was pounding against her rib cage and her breath was coming in short bursts. Remembering the breathing exercises Ed had taught her, she took in one breath, counted to five, then exhaled. Inevitably, she could no longer put off the looming conversation with her dad. A smile played across her lips. He was entirely predictable. She had known he would just appear on her doorstep.

Slowly, she opened the door to see her dad looking sheepish, then gasped as she noticed a woman walking a little behind him.

A lump gathered in her throat. Her eyes travelled down the

long sea-green wool coat to the black ankle boots peeking out as she swished down the path.

Fighting to breathe, Daisy clung to the door. Surely not?

'Daisy, didn't you get my message?' As her dad embraced her, over his shoulder she watched, mesmerised, as the lady stopped and removed her glasses. Then they held one another's gaze.

Letting go, Dan stepped back. Daisy's body became stiff. She could barely move.

'Oh my darling Daisy, I can hardly believe it. To see you after so long.'

Olivia half-ran and half-staggered towards her daughter.

Daisy was frozen to the spot. Randomly recalling something she'd read about how shock could paralyse you, it was as if she was watching things in slow motion from another body. Her mother grabbed hold of her, enfolding Daisy in her arms. The aroma of jasmine filled her nostrils and she was transported to her mother's bedroom. A small, rose-coloured bottle with a puffer on the top. She recalled how her mum would squirt the scent around them both. Holding her as she sobbed like a baby, her father made hushing noises and tenderly guided them both inside.

Standing in the hall, glued together, Daisy still couldn't speak.

'Daisy, Daisy love,' Dan touched her shoulder, trying to coax her.

Daisy could only mumble something incomprehensible.

Finally letting go, Olivia shrugged off her coat.

'Shall we all sit down? It's a shock for all of us,' Olivia suggested.

Daisy nodded and stumbled through to the kitchen. In her head, a dictionary of words spun round in screams.

'I know we should have given you prior warning, but I was so afraid you wouldn't see us if we told you.'

Daisy started to shiver, but her mum was quick to grab and hold her. Leading her to the sofa, she gently sat her down.

'I think you must be in shock. Do you have any brandy or whiskey here?'

Daisy managed to point to a cupboard near the fire.

Unwillingly, she recalled the heady mix of brandy and Tom, a contrast of emotions devouring her.

Olivia began briskly rubbing Daisy's arms to help her warm up. Sitting like a dummy, Daisy allowed her to do whatever it was she was doing. The screams were still echoing in her head. Her mouth had frozen and no amount of screeching in her head could induce it to open. Her dad waved a glass of brandy under her nose. She could hear him encouraging her to sip it.

'It'll help with the shock, Daisy.'

They were busily whispering away to each other, acting as if they were still a couple, little side looks and nuances in their speech. Daisy was mesmerised by them.

She cupped the glass and as she sipped it, the warmth spread through her body.

'I'm sorry too, Daisy. We should have told you, but like your mum said, I was certain you would be resistant. I needed you to see her, to speak to her, to sort this mess out. You do understand?'

At last, with the aid of the brandy, the numbness drifted away and Daisy felt herself fade back into the present.

'I would have resisted, but I accept I couldn't keep making excuses forever.'

'I'm not asking anything from you except to listen to me and give me a chance to explain.' Olivia tentatively put her hand on Daisy's arm.

Daisy noticed the smoothness of her skin, the sparkle of her nail varnish. Sarah would love the colour. But it was the familiarity of her touch that startled Daisy. How many times as a child had her mum comforted her with that same gentle touch?

'I have nothing to give you, Mum. I packaged up anything I felt along with my grief and I put it away.'

The glance between her parents was not lost on Daisy. She was not going to make this easy for them. Turning up unannounced, not giving her time to prepare. Daisy didn't know what to do or say. Rage and joy seemed to be linking arms and clouding her thoughts.

'Oh Daisy, I am so very, very sorry. I know they are just words and they seem so trite, but I mean it. Will you at least listen to what I have to say? After that, you can make your mind up and I will accept your decision.'

Reluctantly, Daisy nodded. 'To be honest, I don't know what to say. All those nights I waited for you to come home. Dad telling me your trip had been extended, until one day he sat me down and told me that the butterfly had flown, and one day it may find its way back to us.' Wiping away her tears with the back of her hand, Daisy carried on, her voice simmering with anger.

'But you never came back, so I got on with my life. There was a hole in my heart that just got bigger and bigger. My writing filled it for a while, until it blew apart a few months ago. It was Sarah who recognised I needed help, then Dad suggested coming here and I've met this guy called Ed. He's helped me unravel my head.'

Daisy immediately caught the look pass between her parents.

'What? Dad didn't tell you I was in therapy? That I was a volcano exploding in front of everyone?' Daisy couldn't hold the frenzy rising in her voice.

'That's what you've done to me! I'm broken! You've both broken me with your lies and secrets. I just want someone to tell me the truth!'

Olivia tilted her head and stroked Daisy's hair. She wanted to knock her away, but instinctively moved into the pressure of her mother's hand.

'You have every right to be angry. I have paid a terrible price for what I did. Your dad did mention that you were speaking to someone. We both bear the blame for the dreadful decisions we made.' Olivia removed her hand and stood up. Straightening her shoulders, she went to stand by the window.

'I worked for the diplomatic service when I left university. In the beginning it was a bit dull, not the high life I imagined. Then one day, I was approached and invited to join a new team being set up to support the military. I was a psychologist and they needed my profiling skills. The excitement I had craved started to manifest itself. The night I met your dad in Paris, I was less than truthful with him. I allowed him to believe he was rescuing me from some errant lover. In fact, I was trying to shake someone who had been following me. He was a dangerous man and I was in no doubt what would happen if he caught me. When we made our life together, I was warned it would never work. But what did those suits know? Love transcended everything - or so I thought. I was an old romantic. The trips away became longer, more difficult. When you came along, I contemplated leaving, but again arrogance got the better of me.'

Slowly turning back into the room, Olivia faced her daughter.

'We didn't account for your dad's growing success. He became very high profile with his writing. In my area of work, he was open to manipulation, and that put you both at risk. I had to make a decision. The caveat we negotiated with my employers meant I could have contact when anything major happened, so your dad could consult me. It was always about keeping you and him safe.'

Daisy sat perfectly still, glancing from one parent to another. The pieces of the jigsaw were not fitting together as she had expected. 'Wait a minute, the diplomatic corps? Dad and Granny Jenny told me you were a psychologist attached to the army. It sounds like you were a spy. No, that sounds too incredible.'

'I take the blame for that.' Dan Tremaine let out a long-held breath. 'When I finally found out the truth about your mum, I wanted to protect you. It seemed easier that way.'

'Truth? What is the exact truth? No more lies.'

Olivia stretched her hand out to Daisy. Knocking it away, Daisy felt her anger begin to bubble.

'What you did was beyond cruel. It was just plain wicked. Abandoning me like that. How could you kiss me goodnight and then just leave? Have you no heart? Why couldn't you have both pretended you were divorcing? Nothing makes any sense. How do I know you are not lying to me now?'

Tears were streaming down Daisy's face. Her heart was fracturing inside her. Such a contrast to earlier, with Tom, when it was bursting.

'I don't know how to make this right,' Olivia pleaded.

'You can't make it right, don't you see that? What's done is done. What is it you want? We make up and act like nothing happened? Play happy families?'

'It isn't about us, Daisy. Your mum has wanted to speak to you for a while. I kept asking her to wait until the book was finished, but then I realised you were in a dark place and that we had caused that. You are absolutely right, we have no idea what we inflicted upon you. What happens next is entirely up to you.' Speaking quietly, Dan stood by the table.

Suddenly Daisy felt adrift, with no compass to navigate what came next. How could she even begin to trust them?

'I've watched your life from afar. Whether you believe me or not, I've regretted every minute of being away from you. When I made the decision to walk away, I truly believed in my heart it was the right one. If we could turn back time, I would never make the same mistake. My own life is on a different path now. It is time for me to put things right, if you'll let me?'

'Are you dying?' It was out before Daisy could check herself.

'My God, no, I'm not dying. Why ever would you think that?' Olivia's voice faltered.

'Isn't that what people mean when they say they want to put things right? Clear their conscience?'

Daisy's head dropped forward. She had expected to be angrier, to rage and shout more. If she was to step out of the shadows, she needed to own her own decisions.

Biting her lip Daisy lifted her head and faced her mother.

'I don't really know what to make of it all. You are both to blame, spinning a web of lies and deceit. How can I trust anything you have to say?'

Looking out of the window, Daisy thought of Tom. A quiver caught in her throat.

'Since coming here, I've made friends. For the first time in my life, I've allowed myself to be open. You have no idea what my life has been like. The continual circus I inhabit. I became more Alex than Daisy. It's like Daisy is trapped in here.' Daisy pointed at her chest. 'Coming here has been the revelation I needed. Discovering Daisy again. Now you both waltz in thinking you can just wipe the slate clean.'

Dan stepped closer to his daughter.

'It's nothing like that. We knew we had to tell you at some point. Then you became so introverted, keeping yourself locked away. When I discussed it with your mum, we decided it was time to put the record straight. You need to tell her Olivia.'

Olivia nodded. 'I'm not dying, Daisy. I did that the day I left you both. I've made a decision to leave the firm. It's time.'

'Oh well then, that's alright. You've made the decision. Do you think that will atone your conscience? Make it easier for you to just pick up the threads of two lives you wrecked? Well, here's a newsflash, I made a decision years ago. I forgot about you. You became meaningless to me. Ed told me it's what people do to protect themselves.'

'Ed?' Olivia whispered, fingering her butterfly brooch.

'Yes, Edward Thornlee, he's semi-retired and he's the therapist I have been seeing. I was doing quite well until now.'

'Olivia, we need to go, this was a mistake. We should have warned Daisy first.'

Straightening her shoulders, Olivia's voice was barely a whisper.

'Daisy all I am asking is for you to listen to me.'

'I feel like my whole world has pivoted on its axis. I can't take it all in.'

Dan picked up his jacket from the back of a chair.

'We'll give you the space you need. We are staying at the pub for a couple of days.'

Dan put his arm round Daisy. 'You find us when you are ready Daisy button.' Kissing the top of her head, he turned to leave the kitchen.

Olivia stared at her daughter's back. Daisy was gazing across the field. 'I'm glad you've made friends, Daisy. Even when you were a little girl it was only ever you and Sarah. These friends sound special to you.'

Yes, they are. They invited me into their lives. One of those friends lives over the hill at the farm.'

'In the dip?' Olivia asked rather too quickly.

'Yes.' Daisy spun round, puzzled by her mum's comment.

'Olivia, it's time we were going,' encouraged Dan.

Daisy made her way to the front door. Mutely, Dan and Olivia followed her.

Olivia kissed Daisy's head as they left.

'Sleep on things and we'll see you tomorrow. By the way, does your friend have a name, Daisy?'

'I have more than one. The guy on the farm is Tom. He's been very kind.'

She noticed a strange look pass across her mother's face.

'I'll see you in the morning.' Daisy shut the door. Leaning against it, she slipped down until she curled up into a ball and rocked herself, weeping as she did so.

CHAPTER TWENTY ONE

'Are you sure you want me here? I mean, this is personal, between you and your family.'

Tom prowled the kitchen, jiggling his phone from hand to hand.

Daisy noted his agitation. After her parents had left, she had spent a good hour or more crying and drinking the remnants of a bottle of wine. She had been very drunk when she had called Tom.

At first, he thought he should call Ed, but Daisy insisted she just needed to rant and get things out of her system. He hadn't wanted to stay. He told her it felt like taking advantage of her, but she was adamant. She needed the physical comfort of another human being. He had helped her to bed, but after she had fallen asleep, he headed to the sofa.

Painfully, Daisy was nursing a major headache from too much wine. She was worried that if Tom left, she would disintegrate and never gather herself up again. Yet deep inside, she knew this was not his fight and she was being totally unfair. Sarah would tell her she was being sappy. She was a wreck. They had done this to her - the two people who should have loved and cared for her the most. Right now, she could only feel hate.

'I know I'm asking a lot of you, Tom, we haven't exactly known each other that long.'

Tom reached out and took hold of her hand.

'I've started to think we were soulmates waiting to meet.'

Moving closer, Daisy pecked him on the cheek. Cupping the back of his head she reached in and plonked a kiss fully on his lips.

'Is this really a good idea now?' Tom stepped back.

'No,' Daisy began laughing. She knew she was verging on hysteria.' Everything is so upside down and crazy. Look at me, how could you ever think I was worthy of your attention? Not even my mother thought I was worth it.'

Tom suddenly pounced forward and grasped Daisy's arms holding her tightly.

Looking up at him, a sliver of fear slid down her spine.

'Stop this Daisy. Stop. I know this isn't you. This hatred will eat you up. True, we haven't known each other long, but I feel like I have known you my whole life. Yet in the time we have spent together I know you are more than this. Don't give in to the darkness in your heart. Do as Ed suggested. Give them a chance to explain what really happened back then. Whatever you decide, I'm through that gate.'

Wide eyed, Daisy looked up into his face. His words were like a smack across her face.

Bewildered, she unfurled herself from his hold.

'Oh my god, I'm so sorry Tom. I am being so selfish.'

'No, you are afraid, I understand. I hate to see you do this to yourself. What was it Ed told you to do? Own your decisions. Own your reactions.'

'You're right. I need to take charge. It was unfair of me to ask you to be here, especially when you have your own family issues going on. It's not your fight.'

'You see, I don't see it as a fight. I see it as a family who need to heal the divisions and the only way to do that is to talk and listen. Only you can facilitate that.'

'You speak as if you know exactly what I'm going through.'

'I do know, my own family has had its wars. It still has them now. Finding the middle ground is the only way to find peace.'

Daisy nodded and capitulated. He was absolutely right. It was time to be the grown up, not the lost little girl. Pulling her fingers through her tangled curls, she suddenly understood. Daisy Tremaine was stuck being ten years old, the age she was when her mother left. She needed to release Daisy from her prison.

'Thank you, Tom. By the way, have you heard from Tabby?'

'A text to say she'll be back by the weekend.'

A knock on the door made them both start. Tom bobbed his head towards the door, giving her a thumbs up at the same time.

'Just remember as frightened as you are, they are the same. You will find the way through.'

Nodding, Daisy went to open the front door. Showing her parents through to the kitchen, Dan stopped mid-stride.

'Ah, Tom, isn't it? Morning.' Dan edged forward and offered his hand. Tom accepted it and was surprised by the grip.

'Dan.'

Standing awkwardly in the middle of the kitchen, neither one knowing what to do or say next, they were saved by the entrance of Olivia.

Daisy gaped at the sight of this slim, dark-haired woman who exuded such confidence. Extending her hand to Tom, a slight colour rose in his cheeks.

'Tom, how lovely to meet to you. I'm so sorry barging in, we didn't know Daisy had company,' she said, letting go of his hand.

'Mum, Dad, why don't you both sit down. Coffee's on and Tom just brought some fresh eggs from the farm. I thought you might like breakfast, it being so early.'

Out of the corner of her eye, Daisy noticed Tom backing away. Her body tensed as she grimaced at how dreadfully she'd behaved. It had been so unfair of her to inflict all this drama on him.

Tom looked at Daisy and gave a confirmatory nod. Clearing his throat, he opened the door.

'I have things to do so it's probably time I left. It's been nice to meet you both.'

Daisy faltered when Tom stepped forward and kissed her cheek.

'I'll see you later,' he whispered. He squeezed her hand to reassure her.

As she watched him march back to his farm, Daisy was aware of movement behind her and turning around, she saw her parents busying themselves making breakfast. They were still in love. How could she have been so blind? Dancing around each other with precision. Her eyes widened as she heeded their smiles and her heart lurched slightly. Hearing her dad's words in her head: 'You are not the only one to hurt.' She had been so self-absorbed, she had never given a thought to them at all. If anyone was looking in now, they would consider them an average family, about to have breakfast.

'Okay, all done, let's sit, shall we?' Olivia seated herself facing the window.

Gathered around the table, Daisy felt as if she had been transported back to the family kitchen. Laughter and arguing over who ate the last rasher of bacon. Falling into the ease of being a family, Daisy's confusion dissipated. Pouring more coffee, she glanced from her mum to her dad. Unexpectedly, she let out a long, contented sigh. She couldn't deny how much she had missed this. More than that, how much she had missed her mum. All her life she had harboured a sickening ache that would never diminish. It had been the not knowing which had fed that ache. How would she bridge her conflict?

Olivia dabbed her mouth with a napkin and slid her plate away.

'I was so glad and relieved you answered my letter, Daisy. It gave me hope. I promise everything I'm about to explain is the truth. It's a complicated package. Let me start with the night I left. It was a big evening for your dad. An award he had worked so hard for. Things had been building the week before and we'd been snappy with each other. I knew he'd had his suspicions for some time about my work. Anyway, I had a last-minute assignment which meant going away the following day, after his ceremony. He was furious, told me he'd had enough and asked me why I had to go away so much. He explained that he'd made some discreet enquiries about me through a contact he had in the defence department. I underestimated his journalistic skills, he always needed to ferret out the truth. Eventually, I had to capitulate, there was no fooling him. My degree in psychology specialised in profiling and I was attached to a military unit, but it was off the grid. A bit like the SAS. He told me he already knew.'

Olivia paused, catching Dan's eye.

'I confirmed your dad's suspicions, then we had an almighty row. He was mad as hell and I couldn't blame him. I had been naïve to think I could live with a foot in both worlds. It was my own mother, your gran, who made me see sense.'

'Granny Jenny?' quizzed Daisy.

'Yes, she was looking after you that night. She heard the shouting and came to see what was going on. I can still see the look on her face. I deceived her too you see Daisy. She knew nothing of what I really did. She thought I was in the civil service. Anyway, your father asked me to be gone by the time he returned from the awards ceremony and after he left, I just broke down. My mother did what mothers do, she held me until I couldn't cry anymore.'

Daisy remained stony-faced.

'Granny Jenny knew, too?' Daisy thought this was too incredible to believe. The deception had spread like a cancer.

Olivia nodded.

'I stayed at her house that night and the following morning, after speaking with your dad, she brought some of my things. Soon after, I left for my next assignment. Your dad refused to even consider working things out. He wouldn't return my calls or let me say goodbye. I thought he might cool off whilst I was away; I thought maybe we could work things out when I came back.'

Olivia looked across to Dan. Daisy watched as her dad nodded his head.

'Your dad said it was too much to cope with and better if I stayed away. It would confuse you too much. Eventually it all became too much for Granny. She was angry with your dad for not trying and cross with me for not trusting her with the truth.'

Looking incredulously from one parent to the other, Daisy struggled to comprehend the web of secrets. The ache deepened as she thought about everything she had missed out on. All those years when she really needed her mum. She was shocked at how easily her dad decided to deny her seeing her mum. This hurt deeper than even her mum leaving. How was she ever going to make sense of it all?

'Dad, how could you do that?'

Dan shook his head and shrugged his shoulder.

'Hearing your mother recount what happened tears me up inside. I was afraid, angry, heck, there are no excuses Daisy.'

'All those nights, I kept asking you when would she be back, at any given point you could have at least let her say goodbye.'

Burying her head in her hands, Daisy had no clue what to say, how to deal with any of this. Lifting her head, she wiped her eyes.

'Thanks to Ed, I have learned that sometimes we bury our memories to protect ourselves or others. Some of the dreams I've been having are vivid dreams of shouting and screaming. I guess somewhere, locked in my subconscious, are the events of that night.'

Daisy pushed herself away from the table and wandered to the window.

'I was ten, for goodness' sake. The woman I relied on, looked up to, loved, just upped and left. You Dad, you just let her walk away. All these years, I thought I had done something, that I had been abandoned. You could have saved me all that heartache.'

Turning to her mother, Daisy clenched her fists.

'Didn't it ever occur to you that you could have written a letter? It was so brutal, so wicked.' Unclenching her fists, she gripped the back of the chair. The years of torment she had suffered, thinking it could have been her fault. Slowly turning from one parent to the other, her heart lurched to see them crying. Inexplicably, a warmth flowed through her. She felt a softening deep inside her.

'There is little we can say in our defence Daisy.' Olivia reached out to take Daisy's hand.

Trying hard not to sniff, Daisy let her mum take her hand.

'Ed told me that the bond between a mother and her child is so deep it can be hard to fathom. I'm not sure I believed him. He explained that it's a primal thing, mothers taking decisions no ordinary being would. You coldly and calculatingly blanked me out of your life. How can you have thought that was acceptable?'

Standing up, Dan straightened his shoulders back. Daisy thought he looked like a warrior setting out for battle.

'Everything you say is absolutely right. Over the years, I've often wondered how I would explain it all to you. There was never a satisfactory conclusion. We both made grave errors of judgement based on our anger towards each other, never considering the impact it would have on you. Nothing can ever change that decision. All those nights I sat downstairs whilst you lay asleep, knowing I was a coward and only thinking of myself. I ran through all the different scenarios of what I… we… could say. I knew you hurt Daisy, every day I watched you shrink a little bit more. When your writing took hold, I was relieved. I acted like a feeble-minded idiot. Instead of facing it, I convinced myself you were going to be ok. I lied again, but this time to myself. It will live with me for the rest of my life.' Dan pulled out his hanky and patted his eyes. 'I still love your mother and hope she can forgive me for giving up on us.'

Olivia went and put her arm around him, comforting him, murmuring soothing words.

Daisy folded her arms and held herself. Her heart ached for her dad. It struck her that when you are in the middle of a crisis, all you see is your own point of view; all you feel is your own pain. But they were all in pain. All of them held in a vice they could see no way out of, other than baring their souls.

'You were, you are, a good dad. You had the guts to stay, when others would have run a mile.'

Her gaze drawn back to the outside, Daisy half smiled. Over the hill was her fantasy. She knew that's all it could ever be. Had she been deluding herself that she could walk away from her life? Turning round, her eyes glassy from tears, she felt something stir within her. These were her parents. They had given her life and yes, they had made a serious error of judgement, but could they salvage anything?

'What do you both want?', she asked, a quiver in her voice.

Olivia faced her daughter.' I know it's a lot to ask, but can you ever forgive us? Invite us back into your life again? No, invite me back into your life?'

Daisy closed her eyes and felt her heart beat against her chest. She had always dreamt of this moment as a child. Now it was here, it seemed less easy.

'You are an adult, Daisy. The little girl I nurtured and loved I left behind. You grew up and I want to get to know the woman you have become.'

CHAPTER TWENTY TWO

Daisy began to clear the table. She was completely at a loss to know how to act. They were asking her to forgive them… was she capable of it? Her dad's part in this was a shocking revelation. Her mother was holding out an olive branch, but Daisy didn't even know if she could accept it. The truth was inescapable, they were all hurting. Then there was Tom, her bright, glittering star on the horizon. What was she going to do about him? He wanted her, she was the one, but was he the one for her? Did she have the energy for a relationship which might prove to be long distance? There was one thing she did know - she owed him an apology for her outburst.

Loading the dishwasher with the help of her dad, Daisy blinked away the image of being in Tom's arms. Pressing *start*, she shut the door before answering her mum.

'You need to give me time to think about all of this. I'm a bit numb from it all. I don't think it's sunk in. Greg is calling me later. I need my head clear to speak to him.' Daisy shook herself as if shedding the coat of another person. She needed to be Alex when she spoke to Greg. Fortunately, she knew part of Alex was still hanging around in the shadows.

Dan gathered his jacket from the sofa, then touched Olivia's arm, murmuring to her.

'We'll check in later, Daisy. Thank you for at least hearing us out.' With that, Dan escorted Olivia from the kitchen and Daisy heard the front door close.

After they let themselves out, Daisy heard her phone buzz and saw it was Sarah.

'Daisy, are you okay? I just picked up a garbled message about your parents.'

'Yes, I'm okay. Mum and Dad have both turned up. I'm a bit

of wreck to be honest. It's like I'm sleep walking or something. I had this sonic boom of hysteria in front of Tom. Oh God Sarah, I am mortified at how I behaved.'

'I'll come over?' Sarah's tone was emphatic.

'Would you? I could do with some back-up.'

'Listen, I'm your kick-ass back-up. I'm on my way.'

Relief flooded through Daisy. No sooner had her call with Sarah finished than her phone flashed again. This time it was Greg.

'Hi, Daisy. I've read through everything and the ending is a stroke of genius. You do realise you have left the door open, don't you?'

'What do you mean?' Daisy felt her brain was in ping-pong mode, flitting from one persona to another without any warning. She hated it when this happened. Daisy sat down on the window seat, the pounding in her chest rising.

'As in, there is another book, maybe even a prequel.' Greg could hardly contain his excitement.

'What? A prequel? Are you mad? I just thought the ending was too predictable and real life isn't like that.' Staring out of the window, she grinned as she watched the lambs jumping in the field. Bentley stood quite still at the fence watching her, his tail flicking away unwelcome flies. In this moment, it was hard to believe the exchanges that had just taken place with her parents.

'You never realised when you wrote that ending that there was another story waiting to be told? A genius and you didn't even realise. There are a few amendments, but I can email those over and then we need to discuss this movie proposition. I wondered...' Greg hesitated.

Letting out a small groan, Daisy moved to open her laptop and clicked on the email. She had inadvertently opened a new chapter in the evolvement of the princess. Why hadn't she seen that? Before she could speak, Greg started talking again.

'Look, I don't want to intrude. I know you're not due back for at least another week, but I want to thrash this out as soon as possible. I'm eager to start the negotiations. Can I come over? I would love to see this place that has fired your imagination. How about I come down on Thursday? My diary is fluid from then until Monday.'

'I don't know, Greg, there's stuff going on, I'm not sure it's a good idea.' Daisy felt her heart pound.

'What stuff? Oh, I get it, you just want to keep this little corner of somewhere to yourself. Come on Daisy, we need to get on top of things.'

Rubbing her head, Daisy had a compelling urge to run. In a flash she'd gone from quiet obscurity and gentle living in Barley Ford to the world crashing in on her. This had not been her intention.

'It's awkward. My parents are here, Greg, both of them. If you come over, you have to keep it to yourself. Tell no one. I mean it.' She inhaled. 'If you do, all deals are off. For good.' She exhaled.

The line went quiet. He was still there, she could hear him breathing.

'Greg?'

'Yeah, I'm here. Wow I don't know what to say. I did hear you right? You said both your parents?'

'Yes, both.'

'I'm confused, your mum is there too? She's come back?' Daisy could almost hear the cogs whizzing in his brain as he tried to unravel the mess.

'Yes and no. I mean, she's here. I don't know, it's a lot to take in. It's complicated. I don't understand either Greg. I'm just trying to stumble through the demolition site that has become my life.'

There was another pause before Greg coughed and continued to speak.

'Bad timing, big style. I don't know what to say Daisy. This is a shock. How can I help? How about I come over on Saturday? At least that way it's on my time and the office don't need to know.' His voice was quieter.

'Thank you. I appreciate it. Life needs to go on, I know that, but it's such a tangle. I'll book you a room at the pub for Saturday night. They do a great breakfast by all accounts. All I ask is that you be discreet. I'm not sure I can face much more just now.' Daisy's lips started to tremble.

'Of course I'll be discreet. I'll see you on Saturday. Call me if you need anything.'

She shut down her phone before anyone else could get her. Grabbing her jumper and pulling on her boots, she headed out across the fields. She needed to clear her head before it imploded.

When she had read about people who gave up the rat race to seek a quieter life, she had never really comprehended what that meant until she came to Barley Ford. She had an impression of rural communities, but little else. They always seemed to be romanticised, as if living there automatically gave you an idyllic life. Since arriving here, she had realised quite quickly that being part of the community was paramount to being able to survive. Dorothy had told her about one very bad winter when they were completely snowed in. Rob had opened the pub as a hub for the villagers. He provided hot meals and a place to feel less isolated. There was a sense of belonging in the way Dorothy explained it. Daisy thought it sounded very comforting.

After leaving her garden, Daisy took another footpath, which skirted along the edge of the farmland, while avoiding the main farm. In the distance she could make out the holiday cottages. After walking for half an hour, she found herself at the bend of the river. Here the water cut through a meadow and rushed along as if it was late.

Daisy found a boulder and sat down. Even though her mind had calmed a little, thoughts still battered away inside. She closed her eyes and breathed in the crispness of the air. The only sounds were scattered bird song and the occasional distant bleat of sheep. With the cascade of water soothing her inner spirit, the pummel of noise was dying away.

As a child, her mother made a big thing of autumn. Preparing for spring was her favourite pastime in the garden. It was the season of hope, she always told Daisy. She revelled in receiving catalogues of bulbs and flowers. 'Time to get the bulbs out,' she would declare. At first Daisy had enquired why Mummy wanted to put lightbulbs in the garden – as it to keep it light for the fairies? Daisy chuckled to herself. She recalled how her mum had taken her hand, walking her through the garden to the old potting shed. There she had shown her the tulip and daffodil bulbs. Daisy could still feel the delight of that moment. Her mum explained how the flowers heralded a new season and the fairies would come out and dance to celebrate.

Remembering the activities they had shared together as a family only added to the strangeness of this whole situation. Everything had been so normal. She never saw her mother sad or crying. There was nothing to indicate the misery that was clearly bubbling under the surface. What did that mean? That she had been genuine in those moments? Or accomplished in her ability to fool everyone?

What must it have been like for her mother to live her life in that way? Two lives so far apart. Yet, in a way, wasn't her own life similar? Her two worlds inextricably linked, but realms apart. Inadvertently, out of her own bewilderment she had created the story of a prince and princess both living dual lives. Sighing, Daisy watched the clouds drift by. There was no way to turn the clock back. What had been done couldn't be undone. Yet she could choose to make the future different. She could attempt to write her own happy ending.

A pheasant suddenly flew in front of her, causing Daisy to jump. Slipping down the rock she steadied herself. A scrunching noise behind her made her twist sharply.

'Whoa, didn't mean to startle you.' A broad grin filled Tom's face.

'What on earth are you doing here, frightening the soul out of me?'

Daisy began to laugh as Jess the border collie jumped on her and began licking her face.

'Looks like I'm not the only one pleased to see you. Some sheep wandered a bit far, I've been rounding them up with Jess.' Tom let out a long low whistle and Jess backed off, sitting herself at the feet of her master.

'Good girl, Jess. When did you discover this little oasis?'

Scrambling off the rock, Daisy crouched down and massaged Jess's ears.

'Literally just now. I had to get out and walk. I turned left and ended up here. It's intoxicating. You know, this place never stops surprising me. How on earth has it managed to remain undisturbed?'

Tom squatted next to Daisy and fed Jess a biscuit.

'People tend to keep it quiet. It's always been the same as long as I can remember, even growing up. Legend has it, this is the glade where the fairies gather in spring to dance and celebrate the return of the light.' A deep, throaty laugh filled the air.

'Back in the day, farmers would come and leave little offerings for them to ensure their crops were safe from disease. It's like you sign an invisible pact to be its guardian and keep it secret. It's been years since I thought about that legend.'

'Sounds a lovely story. You know, this village just keeps on giving surprise after surprise. It's like you never know what will happen next.'

Standing up, Daisy grinned and pushed an errant curl behind her ear. Reaching out, Tom assisted in curling another lock of hair behind her ear, allowing his fingers to trail against her skin. Daisy shivered, but not with cold.

Stepping closer, Tom leant forward and brushed Daisy's lips with his own. Without any warning, he slid his arms around her and pulled her into him.

'I'm sorry about earlier, Tom. I had no right to ask so much of you and I behaved appallingly.'

'There's no apology needed. I'm guessing that as you are here, you have survived. Were you able to rid yourself of that anger? I've been thinking of you all morning, wondering how it all went.'

'I vented a bit, listened to mum tell me her story. The trouble is, I didn't ever think about what happened to them, only me. Things are a little clearer. I'm still mad but not raging.'

Daisy felt a sudden rush of warmth flow through her. She was caught in a landslide of distorted sensations here with Tom. She was gliding on a cloud above the world. When he was near, it was as if nothing could touch her. She wished she could stay like this forever.

Jess barked, breaking the moment and Daisy drew back. Tom frowned, staring back at her.

What's wrong?' his voice heavy.

Shaking her head, Daisy reached out and took his hand. Her own always disappeared into his. Feeling the roughness against her own skin served to remind her how different his world was.

'Tom, I, you are...' the words jumbled around in her head.

'Spit it out Daisy, whatever it is. I can hazard a guess.'

'Can you?' Their fingers interlinked as they stood by the river.

'You are leaving. There is no future, it's all hopeless. It's been a bit of fun, but it's over.'

Agony and ecstasy all in the space of minutes. The wrench was sucking the air out of her. How had he known?

'Tom, when I came here I never imagined any of this, you and me. I've never met anyone like you. To be honest, my relationships have been scant. But there is so much else going on. I have to go back home to Lytton and sort out stuff to do with promoting the book. Your world is here.' Daisy felt the thumping in her chest grow. Why did she feel like she was making a huge mistake?

'Sure, I get that, but don't you think we deserve to try and make it work? Is that all this has been, a fling? A moment of madness? More, importantly, do you want to try? There will always be stuff, issues, other people to consider. But did you ever stop and think about what you really wanted, Daisy, deep down inside here?'

Tom rested his hand against her ribcage.

Trembling, Daisy let go of his hand and stepped back. Jess

suddenly sprang to her feet, wagging her tail.

'I have to go.' Daisy continued to back away.

Tom caught her hand as she moved away from him.

'Don't do this, Daisy, I'm asking you to think about us. I understand you have commitments – so do I. But if you truly feel the way I think you do, then at least give us a chance.'

'It's too much, Tom, don't you see that? Greg is coming over, there are offers on the table, I have decisions to make. They are far away from here. This was only ever a temporary stay. Then there is the situation with my mother. I'm sorry.'

Turning, Daisy began walking, then almost running. She heard him call her name and she fought the desire to turn and race back to him. Her heart began to splinter and she knew deep down she was making the biggest mistake of her life.

CHAPTER TWENTY THREE

By Saturday, Daisy's quiet corner of her new world had been invaded. Sarah was staying in her spare room and later Greg was due to be tucked up in the pub, along the corridor from her mum and dad.

Sarah had arrived late Friday morning and although Daisy was glad to see her, the anonymity she had been seeking began to seep away. The sense of beginning to discover who she actually was rapidly evaporated. See-sawing between Daisy the friend, Daisy the daughter and Alex the author and professional, her head felt like it was in danger of exploding.

Lounging in the garden, enjoying lunch together, Daisy braced herself for Sarah's quips and quizzes. Oddly, they were missing.

'Do you know you have been here five weeks now Daisy? You look as if you have lived here all your life.' Sarah's voice had an unusual seriousness to it.

'It does feel as if I have taken root. However, I need to face the fact that being here was never going to last forever. It was just a pause in proceedings to get myself straightened out.' Stretching out on the lounger, Daisy closed her eyes and tried to blot out her last meeting with Tom.

'And are you straightened out?' Sarah asked.

'I'm in a better place than I have been. For the present, it will have to do.' Daisy took a deep breath and let it out slowly.

The acerbic tone was not lost on Sarah.

'What exactly does that mean? I know you, and if you ask me, you're still all over the place.'

'The revelations about my mum haven't helped, but there is the book and that takes priority.'

Sarah swung her legs round and sat up.

'Resignation then, that's your strategy. You've had a few therapy sessions and wham, you are sort of ok. I'm not buying it Daisy. What about the future? What about Tom?'

'Why do you keep going on about Tom and the future?'

'With everything happening all at once it's easy to be overwhelmed and default to your safe place: the book. Making it the centre of your universe. I'm asking about Tom because I thought he figured in the pecking order.'

Daisy heaved herself up, pulling her cardigan around her shoulders as the clouds covered the sun. Fighting to ignore Sarah's last comment.

'You don't understand Sarah, I have commitments to a contract, whether I want them or not. I don't think I ever thought through what would happen when I had finished the Chronicles. I'm not even sure I ever registered what a circus I had joined. The lack of sleep, the merry-go-round of meetings, interviews etc. I began to ask if it had to be a forever thing. It sounds selfish saying it out loud, I've been incredibly lucky. Don't laugh, but it feels as if I would be dissing the universe if I gave it all up.'

Sarah let out a groan. 'Oh, I think the universe would understand, given everything it seems to have thrown at you. You still haven't answered my question about Tom.'

Daisy's heart flipped slightly. She had been dreading explaining her decision about Tom to her best friend.

'I've finished with him. It all became so intense. And yes, I am all over the place. Meeting Tom was so unexpected, then I realised I was just fooling myself. Mum showing up was a body blow. The book, Greg hounding me about this bloody movie deal – I didn't see how I could squeeze anything else in. Tom belongs here, he has responsibilities. How could I fit into that? How could he fit into my life?'

'Why do you have to fit in? Why can't you thrash out a way of making it work until things die down? God woman, he's gorgeous, kind, caring. He's heaven sent.'

'Funny, that's what he said.'

Daisy dropped her head into her hands. Sarah was right, he was all of those things. He was willing, he had told her they deserved a chance. What was she afraid of?'

Dragging her lounger closer, Sarah tenderly placed her hand on Daisy's shoulder.

'Daisy, if you were writing this, wouldn't you find a way for the lovers to be together?'

'Actually, that's the point… predictable endings.' Daisy's head shot up, her face streaked with tears.

'This is my life and that's the nub of the problem. There are times it's like I'm living a fantasy, with a foot in two different worlds.' Abruptly standing up, Daisy collected the plates and glasses together.

'Daisy, Daisy, why do you think you don't have any choices in this? Sarah stood up.

'All our lives you have hidden away with your words and a life you created for the residents of Ellodin. You created an amazing place with terrific and not-so-terrific characters. But that's all they were; all they are: characters. You are real Daisy. You have a real and wonderful life, you just won't let yourself see it. At some point, you need to let go of the past. From where I'm standing, your mum is trying to do just that. Embrace the very possibility that you have a future.'

'You been in therapy too then?' Daisy skittishly retorted.

'No. I don't need therapy, I know you. Think about what I have said. I'm off to see Dorothy. I've brought some books she asked for.'

Gathering up her things, Sarah walked into the cottage leaving Daisy standing, a little shocked by her friend's comments. Wandering back to the kitchen, she placed the dishes onto the counter.

Musing on an idea, she picked up her phone and called Ed.

'Daisy, this is a surprise. How are you?'

'Oh, you know, up and down. Listen, I know this is a real imposition but is there any chance you are free now? I could do with a sounding board.'

She recognised the hesitation.

'It's cheeky, I know. If you are busy, it's fine. I shouldn't ask.'

'Give me fifteen minutes. I'll be in the garden. Come through the side gate.'

Daisy had never known fifteen minutes feel so long. Ambling down the adjacent lane, she reached the side gate of Ed's cottage and let herself in. There was something scintillating about stepping into another person's private world. Once again, she was drawn back to the garden she knew as a child. Sundays were the day her mum would spend mostly working in the garden, always declaring it was the one part of her world where she felt peaceful. She supposed the garden had been her mum's sanctuary when she was home between trips.

As Daisy reached the end of the passageway which led to the garden, she was dazzled to see what lay before her.

A slate grey patio went the full length of the cottage. Lined with pots, she spotted Ed sitting on a large wicker chair. A jug of juice and glasses were on the table.

'Daisy, you found me. Come in, please, sit down.' Ed pointed to an equally large cushioned chair.

'Ed, this is wonderful. It's like being transported to somewhere very special.'

Slowly sitting down, whilst all the time trying to take in her surroundings, Daisy smiled.

'I'm no gardener Ed, but this is fabulous.'

Ed poured Daisy a drink before settling himself down.

'Thank you. It's been years in the making and no garden is ever really finished. But you didn't come here to talk about gardens. You mentioned running something by me.'

Sipping her drink, Daisy dragged her mind back to the reason for being here. It struck her that even though Ed was semi-retired, he was still very professional.

'Yes of course. You've probably heard my parents have turned up unannounced. I was ambushed. I behaved like a hysterical shrew, shouting and screaming.' Daisy waited, expecting Ed to make a comment, but instead he just nodded.

'Sarah's here, reminding me I'm an idiot, and I'm expecting my agent Greg tomorrow. Not such a great escape after all. To top it all, I have been a bit hysterical with Tom and I think we can safely say I have burned that bridge.'

Ed twisted in his seat. 'Great escape? Ambush? Burning of bridges? It sounds like you are in a war.'

Daisy sat forward. 'A war, I suppose it feels like that.' She rubbed her hands together. She sounded like a spoilt brat again.

'Sarah told me I need to let go of the past. She thinks it's spoiling my chances with Tom. That I'm trying to hide in the world of Alex again. I've told him it won't work between us. So why do I have this sinking feeling that I'm making a mistake? How do I say to my parents "Hey, it's ok, look, I'm not damaged. It's fine you lied to me for half my life? Oh, and by the way, I forgive you". And "Yes Tom, let's give it a go, whatever *it* is, even though you live here and I live in Lytton".' Daisy's eyes began to sting.

Sitting forward, Ed took off his glasses and rubbed the bridge of his nose.

'Daisy, pause and take a breath,' Ed said softly. 'Slowly take it in and slowly exhale.'

Moving her hands into a prayer-like position, Daisy closed her eyes and did as she was instructed.

'Good. Better?'

Daisy nodded.

'What do you really want?'

Daisy tilted her head from one side to the other and scowled. 'Want?'

'To give up Tom? Forgive your parents? Let go of the past? Still write?'

Daisy heard his words and closed her eyes. Exactly what did she want? In all of the things that had occurred since coming to Barley Ford, she had never stopped to ask herself that. She knew she wanted to be Daisy, but what about the rest of it? What did Daisy actually want?

Opening her eyes, she answered in a small voice.

'I don't know.'

Staring down the garden, Daisy shuddered.

'I can't see where your path goes. It just disappears as my eyes follow it. It curves out of view and then nothing. It's a bit eerie.'

Ed suddenly sat up.

'How about we take a walk and see?' He pointed in the direction of the steps from the patio.

Hesitantly, Daisy stood up and wound the long, faded blue scarf she had taken to wearing around her neck. Following Ed, she walked slowly behind him, taking in the variety of plants. She stopped at the rose climbing up the archway and bent over to smell it.

Its delicate vanilla fragrance captured her senses and she was transported somewhere else.

'The scent is so beautiful,' Daisy commented.

Reaching the curve of the path, Ed stopped.

'In honour of my mother. She was an obsessive gardener, among other things. She always believed a garden should have a rose. So here we are, at the point of not knowing what is before us. What is going through your mind?'

'Apprehension, a little excitement, trepidation.'

'Do you want to go first?'

Bobbing her head, Daisy went in front of him and followed the twisting path.

'Oh my God, it's stunning.'

Joining her in the open space he had designed, Ed watched as Daisy wandered from plant to plant and let her hands run through the grasses on either side of the path. She spun round to face Ed. She felt like a child seeing something unexpected for the first time.

'It's so beautiful.' Daisy bent over to smell another rose.

'That's it, I get it, Ed. I really get it. We don't know what's round the corner. We have to hope it's not the bogey man waiting. We have to hope it's something else. Something greater,' Daisy declared.

She ran up to Ed and threw her arms around him, hugging him.

'Thank you, thank you so much for sharing this.'

Staggering back, Ed stiffened with embarrassment.

Daisy jumped back.

'Oops! I'm sorry. I shouldn't have done that. Please, I'm such an idiot.'

He reached out and took her hand, his voice tender and soft.

'Sometimes we need a visual prompt. I'm sure we all know about running away. Trying to escape memories, situations. I bet if you did a survey of folks in this village, they'd all say the same. It's a way we protect ourselves, and for you it was your writing. There is no need to apologise, I'm glad it helped.'

He turned to make his way back. Daisy followed, trying to make sense of what was whirring around in her head.

Seating themselves back on the patio, Ed spoke first.

'Now, you've distracted yourself long enough. How about you take a bold step?'

Daisy leant forward; her hands planted on her legs.

'Bold step?'

'Yes, why are you really here?'

A wry smile played at the edges of Daisy's mouth.

'I was literally paralysed with shock when I saw Mum. After all these years of conjuring up scenarios in my head, the fact is, I never saw this one. Over the years I have been able to blot out her betrayal and I didn't understand why, until I spoke to you. Then I went and changed the ending of the book and without realising it, I have unleashed a whole new concept. Apparently, my agent Greg is so excited at the prospect of a movie and where my writing can take me next. Add Tom to the mix and I'm all over the place. I didn't come here expecting to meet someone and feel the way I do. I'm overwhelmed. Suddenly, I realised that I can't hide. Mum appearing from out of the blue has wiped away any chance of that.

'Tell me about seeing your mum for the first time.'

Daisy fiddled with her scarf.

'Like I said, I was rooted to the spot. I have read that sometimes people freeze when they're in a state of shock. All these sensations were pouring through me – I wanted to scream at her, rage at the injustice, but I couldn't. Bizarrely, I also wanted to rush forward and hug her but I just stood there, immobilised. It was as if I was outside of myself, watching the scene unfold.'

'Where are you at now?'

'I still can't get past the fact they hid the truth. They lied to me and I was only a child! She told me that Dad wouldn't let her say goodbye. How cruel was that?'

'You were a child, now you are an adult. Tell me, in your book, does the princess finally forgive the prince?'

Daisy sat up. 'What?'

'If I recall, there was some issue with trust and the princess took the moral high ground. Did it resolve itself?'

'Yes, the situation resolved itself to a point.'

Ed sank back in his chair and regarded Daisy.

'I have reflected that at times your life was a parallel to the world of Ellodin. It seems you have reached the same conclusions. If you came here in the hope I would tell you what to do, I can't do that. This is your dilemma. You mentioned Tom during this conversation and yet he seems to have melted into the background. So, ask yourself Daisy, what is the primary force here? Forgiving your parents? Ignoring feelings you have developed for Tom? Frustration that you can no longer hide? Is it so scary to consider stepping out into the light?'

Stroking her cheek, Daisy stared back towards to the winding path. Tom, dear sweet, gorgeous Tom. How her heart was yearning for him.

'I'm afraid it's too late for Tom. I have shot that arrow well and truly from my bow. We have no future. Our worlds are so different, how would it ever work?'

'Sounds very final. So, you are still hiding. Protecting yourself, just in case.'

For a brief moment, Daisy heard a frustrated tone in Ed's voice. Abruptly, she stood up.

'Ed, you have been very kind listening to me. Offering me soundbites and trying to help me through this. I'm not sure I would have made it this far without you. But I don't think I'm ready for the light just yet.'

Without warning, Ed stood up and strode towards Daisy.

'I don't give soundbites. I offer reflection and a way for you to question yourself. I rarely give my opinion. It's not how I work. However, in this instance, I am willing to overlook that. So here goes: I think you are afraid. No, I know you are afraid. In the same way your mother was afraid and look where it got her. Empty, alone and lost.'

Ed held his hand up as Daisy was about to interrupt.

'Hear me out. She wasn't any of those things in the beginning. At the start, she took a chance, against all the odds, in a system that doomed her to failure. She and your father made a future. If they hadn't taken that chance, neither one of them would have discovered the depths to which love can reach. You would not be here. Even when the difficulties became apparent, their love superseded everything. If they really hated each other do you think your dad would have stayed married? Your mum watched you from afar, they made a pact to keep you and your dad safe. So here we are, the circle is complete. Fear often drives us to sabotage our own happiness. You and Tom have a chance, the decision on how it will move is in your hands. Shadows or light, I suspect Tom has made his choice.'

Daisy stood perfectly still, rocked by Ed's words.

'You sound as if you know what my mother went through.'

Ed shuffled his feet. 'I know people, Daisy. It's my job. You have a choice. It's the consequences of the choices you must decide about. I trust that was a big enough soundbite.'

Meekly, she reached up and kissed his cheek.

'I know that was out of order, but thank you. That was a majorly kick-ass soundbite. Thank you.'

If Daisy had not been so lost in Ed's words as she walked away, she would have turned to notice a hint of a smile play across his lips.

CHAPTER TWENTY FOUR

Greg drummed his fingers on the counter top in the kitchen. 'Good job you sent me the directions, I would never have found this place otherwise. Talk about off the grid. There's no mention of it on any maps, it completely confused the satnav. How did your dad discover this place?'

'Oh, you know Dad, he's not an award-winning travel writer for nothing.'

'That Rob's a character. Have you seen some of those tattoos? Not your typical country pub landlord. Anyway, here I am.' Greg leant against the breakfast bar.

His crisp shirt, navy tie and steam-pressed suit trousers looked so out of place, thought Daisy. She momentarily pictured Tom in his torn, checked lumberjack shirt, faded ripped denims and his wellies. A wistful sigh escaped her and she shook the thought away.

'Anyway, it seems to have worked some magic on you. I have to say Daisy, you are glowing.'

Glowing, now that she found hard to believe. Daisy wandered over to the table and tried to avoid looking out of the window.

'Are we likely to be interrupted by the parents?' Greg asked hesitantly, joining Daisy at the table.

Daisy opened her laptop and slid onto the chair.

'Not nervous are you, Greg?' She grinned.

'Confused. I thought your mum had run off with a soldier and never wanted to see any of you again. Any chance you can enlighten me?'

Daisy glared at Greg.

'Where on earth did you get that from?'

'You told me she was attached to the military and she

disappeared into the night. I just put two and two together.'

'Made eight by the sound of it.' Daisy wondered how much she should divulge to Greg.

'I filled in the dots. So go on then, what's the story?' Greg sat back in his chair, waiting.

'You're kind of right. She was a psychologist attached to the army. Turns out, it was a bit more elaborate than that. I don't know all the details yet, but she was offered some *under the radar* work abroad, under the premise she was with the diplomatic service. Things got prickly and she was worried about how things would impact on Dad and I. It was tough on them both and they made a decision to go their separate ways. What has surfaced is that she kept in touch with Dad, on and off. Her position has changed, and she has come back to explain her actions.'

Daisy amazed herself at how economical she was with the truth. Maybe it was a family trait.

'Sounds a bit bizarre if you ask me. What happens now?'

'We are still working that bit out.'

'Is this going to impact on things? I mean it's heavy stuff, Daisy. Do you need time out? It might be tough to swing but I can try.'

'I'm not sure that will help me. Keeping busy is a good distraction. I guess as a family we need to keep talking and it will take a while. I still have a few things to work out.'

Eventually, a broad grin broke across Greg's face.

'I have to admit, I am relieved. This is such an exciting time for you. There are so many options on the table. Hey, you could write your parents' story. Now that is worth a movie deal. Dress it up a bit, careful not to ruffle feathers in high places, but it could be a sensational story.'

Daisy burst out laughing.

'Greg, that was not the reaction I was expecting, but why am I not surprised? How about we just deal with the Chronicles first? Then I am definitely taking a holiday. When I have completely binged on unhealthy food and drink, maybe we can talk again.'

Unexpectedly, Daisy had a rare quiver of excitement, the sort she had experienced in the beginning of her writing career, when writing was a thrill. The empty page and the words swirling around her brain. She felt exposed and vulnerable, but at the same time, filled with hope. The prospect of penning a new story; something completely different.

Out of the blue, Greg lunged forward and threw his arms around Daisy.

'My God, you are brilliant Daisy. You've pushed open another door. This is going to sky rocket among the readers, it's genius.'

Extricating herself from his bear-like hug, Daisy began laughing.

'I am a genius and I didn't even know it. Seriously though Greg, you have to calm down. You can't tell anyone about my parents. Seriously. It's all very hush-hush and I would hate the men in suits to take you away one night,'

She couldn't help smiling to herself as she watched the colour drain from his face.

'Seriously Greg, it has to be strictly under wraps. But I may have exaggerated the men in suits.'

'You have had too much country air, lady.'

Daisy took a deep breath, was she ready to explain everything to him?

'We should celebrate, Daisy. I was beginning to worry you were never going to come up for air and deliver on time. Joking apart, I wish I had known you were in such a dark place.'

'Some things are very personal, and why would you? After all, you are my agent and my editor, and there are boundaries.'

Daisy rose from her seat and walked over to the window, folding her arms around herself. It was easier to explain if she didn't have to look at him. The sight of Bentley waiting patiently by the fence brought a smile to her face. Briefly she wondered if Tabby had surfaced.

'My head was a mess. If I am perfectly honest, I was getting a little bored with the prince and princess. They weren't going anywhere. They were stuck. I'd had these awful dreams and flashes of memory from when I was growing up. It was upsetting. Over the years, I have buried all thoughts of my mum. It was too painful. When my dad suggested I come here, I wasn't sure. But it's been enlightening. I have discovered parallels between Ellodin and my own world. Lies, deceit, uncertainty.'

Daisy massaged the back of her neck, it felt right to be explaining things to him now.

'No one can dispute your life being a minefield, Daisy. I still wish you'd had the faith in me to talk about it all. We could have worked something out. I just thought you were suffering with writer's block.'

'Since coming here, my life has unravelled in a spectacular fashion.'

Turning around to face Greg, Daisy felt a tug at her heart.

'If it's cards on the table, I have some news. I've met someone. At least, I had.'

She watched as he sat up. Looking intently at her, Greg encouraged her to carry on. Turning back to gaze out of the window, Daisy continued.

'He's called Tom, Tom Weaver and he owns the farm just over that rise.' Daisy pointed as Greg stood up and joined Daisy at the window

'Unexpected. We've been spending time together. He's been very kind. I never thought about meeting anyone, well not after the last idiot.'

'Exactly what are you trying to tell me, Daisy?'

'I guess it would be the fairytale ending. Rugged, muscular farmer, the handsome hero carries off the damsel into the sunset. The convenient ending, wrapping everything up.'

'Why do I get the feeling there isn't one?'

Greg moved closer to Daisy and put his hand on her shoulder.

'We have known each other a long time Daisy. You are an amazing storyteller, yet telling your own story seems to be where you're faltering.'

A small moan escaped Daisy.

'The princess didn't want to relinquish her kingdom to some prince she had only just met. She wanted to feel the wind on her face and the sand beneath her toes. How about that for a cliché? In being here, I have stumbled across love, real love, for the first time, but I haven't lived my life as Daisy. I have been caught up in the world of Alex and she's suffocated me. If I have learned anything from the events of the last few weeks it's that we only get one shot at this life. We can't waste chances when they are presented. What I'm trying to say is, I need a major plan to allow me to start exploring the world, living my own adventure.'

'Then I guess we need to discuss how we move Daisy and Alex forward so they can find their path independently. Placate those who want decisions immediately and turn things around. How about that for starters?'

CHAPTER TWENTY FIVE

By the time Saturday had rolled into early evening, Greg and Daisy had finally come to an amicable arrangement regarding her future. Daisy had been pleasantly surprised by Greg's willingness to compromise, thrashing out the length of time she could take out, and staving off prospective promotional opportunities.

'I've never told you Daisy, but when we first met, it should have been my boss who was on that judging panel. Daniel was taken ill with food poisoning and couldn't make it. He was very nervous about sending me. I'd only joined the firm a few months earlier and was still very inexperienced.'

Daisy was astounded. 'Crikey, I would never have guessed. Fancy that, we were both newbies.'

'I'm convinced that if the other judges on the panel had been dealing with Daniel, you may well have won. In my gut, I knew you had a winning story, but I was a bit in awe and looking back, I think they used my inexperience to override my opinion. I will always be grateful to you, you launched my career as well as your own.'

'Wow, I had no idea. It all worked out in the end. I suppose we are eternally grateful to each other. Daniel's agency has certainly grown.'

'That's why I am happy to meet you half way in your request for the changes. In all that has happened Daisy, you have never complained, you have been professional at all times. No one would ever suspect all the crap going on in your life.'

Agreeing to meet for Sunday lunch in the pub, she waved him off from the front gate. Daisy was amazed at the sense of achievement and wellbeing flowing through her. It's true, she thought, as she walked back down the path, you never really know what the backstory to people's lives is. Who would have thought Greg was so green at the start of her own journey? At long last, she genuinely felt she was beginning to have some control over her future, Daisy's future.

Sarah appeared at the bottom of the stairs.

'Was that Greg leaving? I disappeared to my room to leave you both to it.'

Walking into the kitchen, Sarah spotted the champagne.

'Oooh, is that champers? Shame to let it go to waste,' Sarah laughed, pouring herself a glass.

'What's next then? I must say, Greg seems a really cute guy. How about we go over to the mysterious pub and keep him company?'

Daisy shook her head as she gathered up her things from the table.

'I'm drained and all out of being sociable, but don't let me stop you. I did suggest we met up for lunch tomorrow in the pub. It's been a helluva day.'

'I've been tinkering with the web page, why don't we post his pic on the blog? Do a bit of a profile on what an agent actually does.'

'That's a brilliant idea. I'll tell you something else I've been thinking about - the Women In Unity group. They are all so committed to their writing and expressing their feelings, how about we post more info on the process of writing and how to become published? It would have helped me when I was starting out, particularly with creating characters. Maybe even a competition? How about you wander over and keep him company, drop it into the conversation? Nice one Sarah, thank you.'

Sarah raised her glass and mouthed cheers.

A knock at the front door resulted in long groan from Daisy. Opening the door, glass in hand, Daisy was met by her mum's beaming face.

'Wondered if you fancied a walk Daisy, just us?' Noticing the glass in Daisy's hand, Olivia smiled.

'Unless I'm interrupting something?'

'Let me get my jacket,' Daisy answered, rolling her eyes.

Sauntering down the lane that led to Weavers Farm, Daisy was battling with an inner desire to link arms with her mum, but couldn't quite bring herself to do so. How was she ever going to get past the hurt lodged deep inside her? It just wouldn't shift.

'What do you think of Barley Ford, Daisy?', her mother asked as she guided her down a hidden track through the trees.

'Quaint. Er, where are we going? I'm not sure this is even a public footpath,' Daisy asked, concerned.

'Oh, it is, bear with me. I want to show you something. Anyway, is that all you can say? It's quaint?'

Daisy gave a roll of her eyes.

'Well, it's tucked away and hidden and that's intriguing. I can't believe it hasn't been discovered and overrun by tourists wanting to forest sleep, or tramp around the countryside.'

'Forest sleep? Whatever is that?'

'You lie amongst the trees and commune with the natural flora and fauna of the forest. Apparently, it is very restorative. Big in Japan, I believe.'

Olivia laughed brightly. 'Well, that's a new one on me. I guess this place has as much to offer in a similar way. Come on, it's just through here.'

Following her mum, Daisy was curious to know where they were going. Pushing the tangle of brambles out of the way, she wished she had put a thicker pair of jeans on.

'Is this even wise, roaming through the woods in the evening?'

Pausing to answer, Olivia shook her head.

'Daisy, one day I will have to sit you down and talk you through some of the situations I have found myself in with work. Don't fret, we are perfectly safe. It's nowhere near being dark.'

Shaking her head, Daisy continued to follow on behind her mum. She silently mused how little she knew about her, and yet there was an ease between them, as if they did this all the time. How was that even possible when a few days ago she was raging with anger over her mother's behaviour?

As they forced their way through the tangle of foliage, it gave way to a clearing surrounded by trees and high limestone cliffs, the evening sunshine penetrated the foliage to shimmer on a natural pool. It was even more beautiful than the one she had discovered the day Tom had appeared. Her heart sank a little as she recalled the events of that meeting.

'Oh my this is – it's beautiful. How did you know?'

Olivia shrugged of her coat and wandered over to a small jetty which protruded out across the water.

'Come and sit by me.' Olivia lifted her face to the dimming sunlight and closed her eyes.

'It's a disused quarry. Nature has reclaimed it.' Olivia spoke without opening her eyes.

As Daisy sat by her mother, she noticed the dark circles under her eyes, the little flecks of silver weaving through her hair. Just as she had been made aware of her dad ageing, so she was with her mum.

'It never stops surprising me, that's what I think of it.'

Olivia's eyes flashed open. She kicked her legs as they hung off the end of the jetty.

'I came here after all the hullabaloo. This place has been a sanctuary for people in my line of work since the war. Weavers Farm for instance, aside from the history attached to the estate, during the second world war it was given over to soldiers who needed to recover from their injuries. The mainstay of the residents are villagers here who have been here for generations, probably from the days it was a working estate. But it has evolved into a retreat of sorts. A place of solitude, with no interference for worn out, stressed operatives to unwind and take stock.'

Soaking in her surroundings, Daisy watched as the wings of dragonflies shimmered when they were caught by shafts of sunlight, or an occasional bird flew by. In amongst the tranquillity, it was hard to imagine the deep need of a person wanting to hide away. Yet she was one of those people.

'I have been very selfish Daisy, I know that. I tried to deny it at first. Even when I met your dad, I was thinking of myself and. how to escape the man who was trying to harm me.'

'Not sure escaping a psychopath is selfish, Mum.'

'Spinning the yarn to your dad and carrying it on was. Imagine if I had told him I was escaping an assassin? He'd think I was crazy. Not to mention what my boss would have said. Anyway, as things developed between us, I realised there was no going back.'

'No going back?' Daisy proffered.

'As in, I grew very fond of him, your dad.'

'Fond? As in you didn't really love him?' Daisy frowned. 'Was there someone else?'

Olivia half smiled. 'I did love… do love your dad. There was someone else before I met your dad, but it began to get in the way. My career was more important. I was very ambitious. My parents worked very hard to allow me to have a good education. I think part of me always wanted to ensure they were proud of me. To know they hadn't wasted their sacrifices.'

Daisy shuffled along the edge. 'It's not unreasonable to want to make your family proud. The thing is, why the change now? I get everything else. I have tried to understand your processes and why you both did what you did. But why bother coming back at all?'

'Last year, I barely passed my physical. Nothing desperate, but I realised that you can't chase bad guys forever. I had to have a psychological evaluation, which is normal procedure. The doc told me it was time to address the future. Face the past. Long story short, his words were, "Olivia, you need to sort out your shit and retire".'

Daisy gawped at her mum. 'Succinct, then.'

'Oh yes, they don't mince their words. Anyway, I was given a desk job and after plucking up the courage to speak to your dad, I explained the situation. Told him it was time.'

'Wait, you had to pluck up courage? I thought you two were chatty friends.'

Olivia laughed and stroked Daisy's cheek.

'No, my darling girl, that isn't how it worked at all. I would contact Dan every so often for updates. He hated me doing it. He always asked when was I coming home. I would always answer the same, soon. It was torment for him.' Tears began to slide down Olivia's face.

'I can't believe I have been so cruel to you both. I have no right to ask for your forgiveness. For denying you so much. Your dad has done a fantastic job of raising you.'

Pulling a tissue from her pocket, Olivia wiped her eyes.

Daisy's heart lurched and without any preamble she threw her arms around her mother and they both quietly sobbed on each other's shoulder.

Olivia moved first. Placing a hand on each of Daisy's cheeks, she planted a kiss on her forehead.

'I am really, truly, sorry Daisy. Please believe me.'

A lightness settled on Daisy. The kernel of pain which had been lodged so long inside her had ruptured and displaced itself. She knew there was still a way to go, but the siege was coming to an end.

'I can see that Mum. I didn't think I could ever get beyond what I was feeling. Ed told me I was afraid. I can see that now.'

'Ed? The man you have been speaking to?'

'Yes, he's been so kind and helpful. Ed… well, it's Edward actually, but I call him Ed. He seems more of an Ed… anyway, he's semi-retired here. He is very calm and a deep thinker. I guess you have to be to do his job, ferreting away in people's memories.'

Olivia shivered and let her hands drop. Daisy noticed her mum's body droop.

'You look exhausted, Mum. It's all too much, this emotional tug of war. Come on, I think you need a hot bath. We ought to let Dad know we are no longer in a war.'

Standing up, Olivia stared at Daisy. A pained expression filled her face.

'Is that how it's been? A war?'

'Strange, Ed asked me that. I think I have been at war with myself. However, knowing the truth has helped me lay some ghosts to rest. Time to call a truce and let Daisy into the light, according to Ed anyway.' Daisy shrugged her shoulders and strolled back down the jetty.

CHAPTER TWENTY SIX

After walking her mum back to The Merchant Moon, Daisy retreated to her own bed. Snuggling down under the duvet, she realised she only had a short time left before she returned to Lytton. Thinking back to the past weeks, Daisy knew she had been sleep-walking through the world she called her life. None of it had made sense until she realised it was within her own power to effect the change needed.

A knock on the door disturbed her thoughts.

'Come in Sarah.'

Plonking herself on the empty side of the bed, Sarah sighed.

'What?' asked Daisy, slightly irritated at the interruption.

'You disappear with your mum, then I walk in and you are nowhere to be found. Then I discover that you're up here hiding.' Sarah turned on her side, facing Daisy.

'I'm not hiding, I'm tired,' Daisy's tone rose.

Sarah gave a long, impatient sigh.

'Do we have to do this now? It's late.'

'Yes, we have to do it now. It's like trying to extract state secrets from you. You're not telling me anything. You haven't even asked how my evening with Greg went.'

Rolling her eyes, grinning, Daisy twisted to face her friend. There was no escaping the sparkle in her eyes.

'I'm not being given a chance with your interrogation. Judging by that look of smug satisfaction, your evening must have gone quite well.'

Propping herself up on an elbow, Sarah's face lit up.

'Where have you been keeping him all these years? How come you have never introduced us? He is fabulous. Did you know his mother runs that posh gallery on the High Street in Lytton?'

'No, I didn't know about the gallery. Come to think of it, I don't know much about him personally. Only that he started with the agency around the time of the competition. He explained to me today that it was a pure fluke he was on that judging panel. Fate. I wonder how things would have turned out if it had been his boss? Another example of how self-absorbed I have become. You seeing him again then?'

Laying on her back, hugging a pillow, Sarah murmured 'yes'.

'Guess you have charmed him into agreeing to do a profile for the blog and the website then? I'm thrilled for you. Greg is a sweet guy, even though he thinks he's a tough nut.'

'Enough about me, what about you and Tom? Are you really going to walk away?'

Daisy shuffled up the bed and leant against the headboard. She had been working hard at trying not to think about Tom.

'I don't get how it can work Sarah, he's here, I'll be god-knows-where, back on the hamster wheel. I really thought when I finished the Chronicles that was it. Seems I have opened a whole new can of worms. Or rather, a new storyline. Not to mention this movie idea. I'll be at everyone's beck and call. How do I fit in a relationship, a long distance one at that? He'll be under the microscope as a significant other. That's not fair.'

Sarah pulled herself up and flicked the pillow at Daisy.

'You need to listen to yourself. Why on earth is that a problem? You move here and do all your writing here. What better place to fire those creative juices? You can be so dense sometimes, you know. Anyway, doesn't Tom have a say in that? Where is his choice in all of this?'

'How can I move here? My life is not here. Tom has other stuff going on. You've heard how everyone speaks about this place. It's guarded like a state secret. Imagine if I did move here, it would never work. And anyway, I think I've already burned the bridge with Tom.'

'You are so infuriating, do you know that? Your life can be wherever and whatever you want it to be, idiot. Haven't you reached some sort of milestone in your career, affording you more say over what happens? This is the age of Zoom and the virtual world. Imagine it working as part of your enigma… the mysterious Alex Dennison: a hermit or a recluse? Great marketing ploy. Anyway, isn't it your job to write and Greg's job is to make sure your work is saleable. Then you show up for events? And with Tom, it seems to me that the bridge is only burned in your head.'

Daisy stared at her friend. She had never seen her so fired up. Hooking up with Greg must have stirred her emotions like a whirlwind. Daisy did concede that she had a point. When Sarah spoke about how things could be, it sounded far simpler than when she did. She had never even thought about anything being Tom's choice. She was making the decision for him. Sarah was right, this was a digital age, so many things could be done via the internet now. Maybe there was a way.

'In theory, but you and Dad live in Lytton. I don't even know if I want to move here.'

Sarah rolled off the bed, throwing another pillow at her friend.

'Yeah, that's right, I forgot we live so far away from this place. At least an hour away. Tom has no brains, he can't even think for himself, even though he runs a successful farm single-handed. As for you, well, on this occasion, words fail me. Why on earth are you talking yourself out of this? You're not even giving it a chance to work or fail. You have just made your mind up. Carry on being a hermit, playing it safe and consequently ending up an old maid.'

Daisy was shocked by Sarah's response.

'It's not that simple Sarah.' Even Daisy was struck by the whine in her voice.

'You know Daisy, it's as simple as you want it to be. You are afraid, I can tell. You've shut yourself away, deliberately avoiding relationships. I know what happened with the last guy you were with, he was just after the glory, but don't let him define you. You are in charge of your destiny, isn't that the point of the story of Princess Lilia? It's as if a great excuse has presented itself to you in the shape of movie deals, more books to write. As for Tom, you are not even giving him the chance to fight for you. You have disabled him as you believe you have been disabled.'

Sarah marched to the bedroom door, leaving Daisy open-mouthed at her outburst.

'I'm off to bed. Sleep on it and I will grill you at breakfast. I need one, just one, perfectly evidenced reason why it can't happen. Good night.'

Daisy lay aghast at her friend's tirade. She made it all sound so simple. Was it that simple? Turning out the light, she slid down under the covers. She had closed herself away. Sarah was right, it was easier to continue hiding than take a chance. Drifting off to sleep, thoughts whirled around her brain until eventually she fell into a fitful slumber.

Sunday morning brought a parade of visitors through Daisy's kitchen. Her parents arrived first. Daisy could not mistake their renewed interest in one another and silently offered a small prayer. More for her dad, because she knew how much he still loved her mum and needed her back in his life. She also prayed that her mum wasn't messing about and meant everything she had said. Daisy was still curious about her mum mentioning that there had been someone else. She wondered if her dad knew about him.

Daisy had also watched Sarah and Greg, silently communicating with sweet glances and an odd touch of fingers. She was relieved Sarah had been so engrossed in Greg that she had not revisited the conversation from her bedroom last night. Daisy had been genuinely shocked at Sarah's outburst. Rubbing her eyes, Daisy felt weary. She had slept on and off with various images of Tom's face floating around her. An ache spread through Daisy as his dazed expression swam through her mind, as she relived the moment she told him she didn't think it would work between them.

Suddenly, her quiet contemplation was broken by the familiar bark of Harry. As Daisy checked the garden, she was halted mid-step by Harry dancing around her feet, his bark becoming more and more high-pitched.

'Whatever is the matter, Harry? Why are you on your own?'

'What's going on Daisy?' Olivia had joined her in the garden.

'I'm not sure. It's not like Harry to be out without Dorothy. Come on boy, let's go and find Dorothy.'

'I'll come with you.'

A whisper of dread drifted through Daisy's mind. She quickened her pace and as she reached Dorothy's door, her heart was pounding.

Harry scurried ahead of her and straight through the open front door. Following the little dog, Daisy began calling Dorothy's name. More barking from Harry led Daisy through to the kitchen.

'Oh my God, thank goodness you are here Daisy.'

Daisy almost collided with Tabby, who was on the floor leaning over Dorothy.'

'Tabby, what on earth? Dorothy! What's happened?'

Dorothy was laid on the floor, one of her legs at an awkward angle.

'I'm not sure, I heard her scream and then Harry was frantically barking. When I came downstairs, she was already on the floor. I think she must have been standing on that chair for some reason.'

Daisy followed to where Tabby was pointing. A kitchen chair lay on its side by the dresser.

'Have you called an ambulance?' Olivia knelt down, feeling for a pulse.

'Yes, they are on their way. Sorry you are?' queried Tabby.

Daisy began to feel the familiar pounding in her head. Then remembered to breathe, the last thing she wanted was a panic attack.

'This is my mother, Olivia. She... she's been visiting.'

'You haven't moved her, have you?' Olivia's voice cut through the tension.

'No, she's just as I found her. I'm Tabitha by the way.'

Olivia nodded in acknowledgement.

'Can you find a cushion for under her head? This floor isn't exactly comfortable.'

Obediently, Tabby went to pull a cushion from a kitchen chair and passed it to Olivia. A noise in the hallway distracted them. Harry scampered out, barking again.

'Dorothy, Dorothy, where are you?'

Recognising Gerald's voice straightaway, Daisy stood up.

'In here Gerald, the kitchen.'

Standing in the doorway, Gerald surveyed the scene.

'Dorothy! What happened?'

Daisy watched as Gerald knelt precariously beside Dorothy.

'Olivia, this is a surprise. I heard you were in the vicinity. Checked her pulse, she's still with us?'

'Yes. She's still breathing. Looks to me like she was clambering up on a chair to reach a top cupboard,' Olivia pointed out.

Daisy's eyes slid from Gerald to her mother. They knew one another? A shiver wiggled its way through her body. More secrets surfacing and once again she was the stranger.

'Come on old girl, you can't go down like this, not now.' Gerald spoke tenderly, stroking her limp hand.

'Daisy, would you wait outside for the ambulance? Tabby, how about you take control of Harry before he yaps himself into a coma.'

Both girls stared at each other as Olivia took command of the situation. Daisy was still fixated with the familiarity between Gerald and her mum. Then, as she wandered outside, a light flicked on in her brain. Of course, Gerald had lived here for so long he must have known her mum from when she stayed here. Did that mean Dorothy knew her too? Is that why Dorothy talked to her about forgiveness? The questions just kept on bombarding Daisy and the answers were elusive. It was like being on a merry-go-round that would never stop. Just as she was beginning to work everything out, another piece of the jigsaw eluded her.

CHAPTER TWENTY SEVEN

The inhabitants of Barley Ford had instantly spurred into life as news of Dorothy's accident spread through the village. Keen to offer help of any kind, they had huddled together at her gate desperate for news. As the ambulance drove away, the small crowd dissipated with calls of 'you know where we are. Let us know how she goes on.'

By the time Dorothy had been whisked away with Gerald by her side, Tabby decided Daisy was in charge of Harry.

'He's nearer to you than me. I've never been keen on his snuffling. Poor thing, nature was not kind designing those dogs with squashed faces.' She handed the lead to Daisy.

Daisy was speechless.

'Close your mouth Daisy, it's not a good look.'

'I'm confused, I thought you were in Scotland at your parents' place?'

'I was.'

More questions gathered pace, circulating in Daisy's mind. What had Tabby been doing at Dorothy's?

'Let's talk and walk as they say.' Tabby marched in front of Daisy.

Setting off with a long stride, Daisy trotted to keep up. The whole situation was beginning to irritate her.

'Tabby wait, stop,' Daisy shouted, surprising herself. Even Harry sat down.

Stopping, Tabby paused before turning round. Daisy had the distinct impression that no one ever questioned Tabby, Daisy stood her ground in the middle of the lane.

'What?' asked Tabby, sounding incredulous.

'I am not walking and talking.' Standing with her arms folded, Daisy remained rooted to the spot.

'Tom said you were very determined. Speaking of my brother, what's going on with you two? I was pleasantly surprised when you hit it off. Finally, someone else to worry about him instead of me.'

Daisy's foot was tapping the ground when she stopped, mid-tap.

'What? No, it's not like that. You've misunderstood.'

'Oh, trust me Daisy, I have understood perfectly. Are you telling me then it was just a holiday fling? Was he just your bit of rough on the side?'

Daisy stepped back, feeling the punch of words deep inside her.

'I'm not on holiday and secondly it's none of your business. Anyway, you've no room to talk, flouncing out of your house, leaving your brother worried sick, Dorothy is on her way to hospital and you act like this is just every day for you.'

The two women stood opposite each other. Harry had laid down, sensing disharmony.

Mirroring Daisy, Tabby folded her arms, cocking her head to one side.

'You have no idea what every day is like for me. But then, how could you? Coiled away in your little tower of make-believe with fairy dust and handsome princes. Oblivious to the real world around you. If it wasn't for people like me, you wouldn't have a world like that to inhabit.'

'What is that supposed to mean?'

'No matter. You'll be gone soon what would you care?'

Daisy felt her frustration building. Why did everyone have to speak in riddles?

'Tom didn't tell me what was going on with you two but it upset him. If you ask me, I think he needs you here to help with the farm and the cottages, which I gather were your idea?'

Tabby began clapping her hands. 'Whoa, I'm shocked Daisy, inside that whimsical little heart of yours beats a hard core. Nothing going on with you and Tom? So how come you are so concerned?'

'He's been kind to me, he listened. He's become a good friend.'
Daisy felt a familiar flush rush across her cheeks.

'Well, from where I'm standing it's more than friends. I know my brother and he's hooked. I don't know what's gone on between you two, but he's been mooning about like a lost puppy. Don't mess him about.'

There was a tone of protectiveness mixed with defiance in Tabby's voice. Mess him about and you deal with me. Daisy straightened her shoulders, refusing to be intimidated.

'You still haven't explained why you were at Dorothy's?'

'I don't have to explain myself to anyone and certainly not to you. This has nothing to do with you. Sounds to me like you have washed your hands of my family. Forgive me Daisy, I suggest you sort out your own family issues before you start being liberal with advice.'

Suddenly, Harry jumped up and started dancing around and barking.

'How dare you! You know nothing about my family,' Daisy hit back.

Coming up behind Tabby and Daisy was Olivia.

'Everything okay here ladies?' she asked, stepping between them.

No one answered. Olivia walked over to Tabby.

'How about we head over to the farm, I'm sure your brother will want to know you are home safe and about Dorothy. Daisy, why don't you take Harry inside and I'll join you later.'

Deftly turning Tabby around with an arm on her shoulder, Daisy watched as her mum walked away.

'What the hell just happened there, Harry?'

CHAPTER TWENTY EIGHT

Daisy stomped down the garden path and had barely reached her front door when she heard Ed call out to her.

'Thought you could do with a drop of something to calm the nerves.' He held up a bottle of brandy.

Once inside, she hung up Harry's lead and glanced down at her charge.

'Don't worry fella, she'll be back before we know it.' His whimpers echoed in the hall.

'I'm not sure how long Dorothy will be in the hospital,' Ed pondered as he sipped a brandy.

Daisy was struck by how comfortable he looked, tucked into the armchair by the fireside.

'To think a little squidgy dog like Harry knew to find me? Though I bet it was Tabby who sent him. Is she staying with Dorothy? Bit odd her being there, I'm sure she said she was upstairs. And go Gerald, he was like some towering Captain of a ship ordering us all around. You would think he would have folded into a heap with shock when he stood in the doorway. Get this, he recognised my mother. Now she has taken Tabby back to the farm. It's like she knew them all.'

Curling up in the window seat, Daisy was struck by how everything looked so calm now. As if the veil had come down on the village again. Turning to face Ed, Daisy accepted the brandy he was handing her.

'Thank you.'

Daisy watched as Ed settled himself back into the chair. Swirling his brandy around in the glass.

'Come on Ed, out with it.'

'You obviously haven't been told much about Gerald. In his other life, he was the commander of a special service unit. In fact, he was partly instrumental in setting this whole place up… along with his able assistant, Dorothy. Gerald always believed it was one thing to serve your country but another to be turned out to grass and abandoned. His favourite term was "discarded like trash", slightly dramatic, but you get the drift. He recognised that operatives suffered with PTSD long before it became a thing.'

Daisy stared in disbelief.

'As for Tabby, I believe when she's home, Dorothy's is her go-to place. So, you may be right about her staying. Dorothy has a very nurturing trait and is an extraordinary woman you know. I'm guessing she hasn't shared her story with you either.'

Daisy sat perfectly still, flabbergasted by Ed's disclosures.

'Ah well, it is hers to tell, not mine. Needless to say, this village is unique in its residents.'

'Is that why you are here?' Daisy dared to ask. 'It's none of my business, I know. But my curiosity is piqued now. You seem too lively to be closeted in this time warp of a place.'

Hesitating, Ed took a breath before answering.

'Yes, in answer to your question. Curiosity can be a risky thing, Daisy. We learn things we can never unlearn.'

'That sounds a bit Freudian, Ed. No details then?'

'Another time maybe.' Ed shifted in his seat. 'Are you going to tell me what was breaking out between you and Tabby earlier? I was walking up the lane when I spotted you both in a stand-off. By the way who was that lady with her?'

'Tabby has this superior air about her. She can be very haughty. I told her it was unfair on Tom to keep popping up and then disappearing. I think he needs more help and she is most unhelpful. She was quite insulting. She said something very odd, if it wasn't for people like her we couldn't do what we did, or something like that. You know, the more I learn about this village, the less I know.'

'Tabby is very much her own woman. She is feisty and sharp around the edges. She and Tom are close and she is extremely protective of him. I can understand why you think as you do.

May I suggest you cut her a bit of slack and even try to get to know her.'

'Not sure that is likely to happen. She made it perfectly clear I should stay out of her way. Basically, told me to sort out my own life, rather than dishing out advice on how to run hers. Maybe she has a point.'

'Do you really take things at face value and not look beneath the surface? I thought you had overcome some of your inhibitions. What was it you said? Everyone has a backstory?'

'Fair point. If Tabby puts her prickles away, I'll make an effort. Sarah had a go at me last night. She's decided I'm looking for excuses to continue being a hermit. It's hard when you have lived your life a certain way and then you have to break those shackles. It's daunting.'

'It is, I agree, but if you don't, what is going to change? We have to risk ourselves to find the things we are seeking. Imagine if no one ever got over their first love, would any of us be here?'

Daisy smiled.

'When you put it like that, it makes sense. You are very wise Edward Thornlee.'

Ed batted away her comment with his hand.

'Are you going to tell me who the lady was that led Tabby away?'

'Oh yes, that was the famous absentee mother, Olivia Tremaine. She's something else.'

Daisy watched as the colour drained from Ed's face. Draining his glass, he stood up and helped himself to another.

'Go steady, else you'll be sleeping in that chair.'

'Yes, yes, sorry, it's been a long day.'

Unconvinced, Daisy was about to speak when Harry came in and started padding about her feet.

'Oh God, I'm a terrible dog-sitter, you need feeding. Come on boy.'

Having fed Harry with some leftover chicken, Daisy plonked herself on the sofa and tucked her legs underneath her, sipping the remnants of her brandy.

Ed remained in the same position, unmoving, saying nothing. Instead, he stared distractedly out of the window.

'I think my mum is calling in later, you'll get a chance to meet her.'

Ed continued to stare out of the window.

'Ed what's wrong? Are you even listening to me?'

Jerking his head round, Ed's face looked serious.

'Sorry, yes, I am. I was just thinking about Dorothy. I was hoping Gerald would have been in touch by now.'

'I'm sure he'll call as soon as he knows anything.'

They both jumped at the sound of the front door opening and the call of Olivia.

'Hello?'

'In here, Mum.' How easily it slipped out, as if it was everyday her mother called in.

The door swept open and Olivia appeared, breathless.

'Gosh Mum, are you okay?'

Daisy uncurled herself from the sofa and sat up.

Olivia lifted her hand up to signal she was fine.

'Any chance of a glass of whatever you are enjoying? It's quite a trek down the lane from the farm.'

Unwinding the silk scarf from around her neck, Olivia shrugged her jacket from her. As she dropped it on the chair, she noticed Ed.

Daisy was held in a trance as she watched Ed slowly rise from his chair and Olivia stutteringly step towards him.

'Olivia, it is you?'

Her head bobbing in acknowledgement, her voice was barely a whisper.

'Edward. You came back.'

As Ed held out his hand, Daisy stood mesmerized by the scene playing out in front of her. She continued to gaze as her mother took hold of his hand, while Ed all but knelt and kissed hers.

It was only when Sarah burst through the door that the frozen moment shattered. Daisy wasn't sure what she had just witnessed.

CHAPTER TWENTY NINE

Stopped in her tracks, Sarah looked from Olivia to Ed, then to Daisy. Harry was jumping about, his shrill barks piercing the room.

'Harry, here boy, that's it. Good lad.' Sarah shushed him and, finding the remnants of a treat in her pocket, offered it as an appeasement.

Having calmed the excitable pooch, Sarah called to Daisy.
'Daisy?'

Lifting her hands in the air, Daisy shrugged her shoulders and beckoned her friend to join her.

Completely oblivious to the girls, Ed and Olivia stood staring at each other in the middle of the room.

'What's going on Daisy? It feels like we shouldn't be here,' whispered Sarah.

'You're right, we shouldn't, come on.' Daisy nudged Sarah and they crept out of the room, gathering up Harry as they went.

'What the hell is going on back there, Daisy?' asked Sarah once they were in the kitchen.

'I have no idea, you tell me. Ed came round with a bottle of brandy to make sure I was okay, then Mum turned up and wham! They just, well, froze in the middle of the room. He'd spotted Mum intervening between Tabby and I.'

Sarah's eyes widened.

'We were having a bit of a spat. Anyway, Ed wanted to know who she was. Thinking about it, he did go a bit pale when I told him she was my mum. Plus, you'll never guess what - Gerald set this place up. Turns out he was some sort of commander of a special unit connected to the government. Who knew? I tell you Sarah, I feel like I'm dreaming.'

'It's like they've both seen the same ghost.'

Sarah slowly turned her head to look at Daisy.

'They must know each other.'

'How is that even possible, Sarah?' Daisy started to pace back and forth, agitated by a whirlwind of thoughts.

'Neither of them has mentioned the other. Except Mum called him Edward and said "you came back". What did she mean?'

'It means I know Edward.' Olivia hovered in the doorway.

Both girls turned in unison.

'He's left, by the way. Gerald called him, they are sending Dorothy home and Ed has offered to go and collect them. She's fine. A sprained ankle and shattered pride.'

Daisy fist pumped the air and Sarah yelled, 'Yeah!'

'Go Dorothy, tough as old boots.'

Olivia wandered slowly into the kitchen.

'Mum I think you have some more explaining to do. What's the deal with you and Ed? Not to mention you and Gerald greeting each other like old friends.'

'The edited version is that our paths have crossed a few times with work. Ed is quite renowned in his field. I haven't seen him in years. We lost touch and it was a shock, seeing him here. He often wondered if he would end up here, writing his memoirs. I don't know why it didn't click earlier. Sorry to disappoint, that's all there is to it.'

As she scrutinized her mother's face, Daisy scrunched up her own. This woman was trained to fool people. She had made a living out of being poker-faced. However, the slight tremor in her voice told Daisy another story.

'And Gerald?' queried Daisy.

'Same thing, work-related. This place was Gerald's innovation. He acts as a caretaker.'

'Well Olivia, it all goes on here in this hidden little hamlet.' Sarah sank back in her chair.

The three women were momentarily quietened by their own thoughts. Daisy tilted her head to one side, watching her mum as she knelt down to pet Harry.

'It's a treasure for Daisy's next book, no doubt about it,' stated Sarah.

'Scratch the surface of anywhere Sarah and you'll find a hundred tales waiting to be told. Though I admit, dull can be very appealing. Well ladies, it's late and it's been quite an evening. I'm feeling quite exhausted.

Dropping a kiss on Daisy's head, Olivia blew one to Sarah.

'Night girls, don't stay up too late.'

Hearing the front door close, Daisy lingered by the kitchen counter. Her mind whirling from the last half hour.

'This is becoming very intense,' Sarah mused.

Just as Daisy was about to respond, her phone pinged with a text.

'Well, things just got a bit more intense. It's a message from Tom. He wants to meet me tomorrow. Plus, we are invited for lunch. Including you and Greg. Get this, he's asked Mum and Dad too. Apparently, his parents, Joseph and Genevieve, are visiting.'

Daisy flopped on a nearby chair.

'It's a bit like being summoned to the manor. Genevieve, that's a very exotic name for a farmer's wife. Greg as well? I shall have to use my persuasive powers to make him stay a bit longer. Not that I'm complaining.'

Daisy grinned, 'I'm sure you'll find a way. You know Sarah, I thought my life was an Alice in Wonderland event. But now I'm certain this is all getting much weirder. I haven't even seen Tom since I told him it wouldn't work. Now this. Mum knowing people in the village… it's like being transported to a parallel universe.'

'Your mum was very skittish when she was talking about Ed…' Sarah gave a long yawn.

'Hmmm, I don't think she's telling us the whole story. People do not look at each other like that when they are just colleagues.'

'I am inclined to agree. I'm sure you'll uncover whatever it is. It's weird though, we knew as her as children and that's how we think of her. Yet here she is and it's like we know nothing about her.'

'Yes, it is odd. I suppose we all have to get to know one another again, warts and all.'

Daisy stared at her phone.

'Why do you think Tom wants to see me? How on earth can I go up there and have lunch?' Daisy uttered.

'Maybe he has decided to leave the manor and run away with you. You need to go. Hell, I am not missing lunch at the manor. Anyway, I'm exhausted, it's all far too much for my little head. Here's me thinking you'd be bored here and desperate to get back to Lytton. Just goes to show. Anyway, I'm off to bed.'

Giving Daisy a hug, Sarah yawned again.

'Yep, I'm all done in. Night, girlfriend.'

Waiting until Sarah had gone, Daisy quietly opened the back door and lifted her head to the night sky. Thousands of stars were visible with no light pollution to dim their brightness. The tension had been palpable when her mum had walked in. The look on Ed's face was priceless. Daisy admitted she recognised love when she saw it. She'd never seen her mum look at her dad in the same way.

An image of Tom gazing at her entered her mind, causing a slow warmth to flow through her. Was it a good idea to meet him? How could she ever face him after everything she'd said?

Harry came and plonked himself on her foot.

'Oh Harry, I don't know what to make of anything. I do want to see him. I've missed him. Perhaps Ed and Sarah have been right all along. I have to listen to him, let him make his choice. Do you think it's possible, Harry, for Tom and I to find a way through the obstacles?'

Bending down to stroke him, Harry gave a little squeak.

'Missing Dorothy are you? She'll be home soon. I miss her too. I have a feeling she would have just the right answer. Come on, bedtime.'

Daisy closed and locked the door and, picking Harry up, she went upstairs to bed. Her mind was awash with thoughts. The pieces were slowly beginning to fit together, and she fervently prayed that her mum wasn't about to break her dad's heart again.

CHAPTER THIRTY

Daisy dragged one foot in front of the other. Tossing and turning in bed last night, she had relived every meeting between Tom and herself. Each one building on the intensity of two people who were clearly drawn together. Since the arrival of her mum, everything had become garbled and Daisy still felt like she was falling down a rabbit hole.

It was an airless morning as the apprehension within her grew. Part of her couldn't wait to see Tom, yet she felt it was just prolonging the inevitable. He had suggested the spot by the river where he had startled her when out searching for his sheep with Jess. She smiled to herself, remembering how friendly his sheepdog was.

As she approached the clearing, she could see Tom perched on a boulder, throwing stones into the river. Standing for a brief moment, she drank in his outline. Her eyes lingered on his broad shoulders and the way his hair gathered in a clump at the nape of his neck. Stirring the memory of her caresses across his sun blemished skin, she let out a long sigh. It suddenly dawned on her that she knew every inch of the figure before her. Those intimate moments enfolded her, melting her very core.

'You going to stand there all day, or come and sit down?'

'How did you know I was here?' Daisy smiled to herself, a longing coursing through her.

'I'm a man connected to my surroundings. I hear things most men don't.'

Standing up, Tom turned around, a large devilish grin spreading across his face. The ache in Daisy stretched like a chasm.

'I was afraid you wouldn't show up.'

'You have Sarah to thank. She told me I was being selfish

making decisions for us both without giving you a chance.'

Before Daisy could say anything else, he wrapped his arms around her, burying his face in her hair. Daisy's legs buckled and she welcomed the tangible excitement pulsating between them.

After a brief moment Tom gently stepped back, combing her curls away from her blushing cheeks.

'Daisy, we need to talk about us.'

'What us, Tom? Is there an us?'

Taking her hand, Tom led Daisy to the boulder he had been sat on.

'I think that is the wrong question. Maybe it's more whether you want an us?'

If the feelings coursing through Daisy's veins now had been anything less intense, she would have found an excuse to stamp on Tom's toes and run away. The mesh of netting which had enveloped her heart was beginning to weaken. After so long of denying herself a life, she had a chance to find out what being in a relationship could mean. Like Princess Lilia, she needed to do this her way.

Gazing intently into Tom's eyes, Daisy's world tilted on its axis.

'I want to believe there could be a future, I really do. But so much has happened in short space of time. Mum turning up with her bizarre story has complicated things. I was beginning to think I had it all sorted. You are so connected to this place and let's face it, life here is not the usual run-of-the-mill existence.

'I get all of that, but what does your mum turning up have to do with us?'

Daisy found herself clutching him to her. She could feel his breath against her face. Tom was like a fortress surrounding her.

'I have no answer.'

'Living here is different to the world you live in. I did tell you I was no good at this stuff, I'm not even sure what I'm trying to say. Except there are choices and ways to work things out.'

A look of hope glistened in his eyes. At that moment, the sun disappeared behind a cloud and Daisy shivered.

'Are you saying you would leave here?'

'No, not exactly. I'm asking does it have to be either or? How long have you been here now?'

Daisy closed her eyes and breathed in the fresh, damp air. She could have lived here all her life, that's how connected she felt to this place.

'Long enough to know it will be hard to leave.'

'So don't leave. Make this your home and when you have to travel then go, but otherwise...'

Tom left the words in the air.

Staring at him, she was caught in the treacly pools of his eyes. She had no argument that could be sustained. In that moment, she knew that she loved him, heart and soul.

'I've been a fool. I never imagined I would ever meet anyone who could make me feel the way you do. I'm a little scared. Not to mention overwhelmed by how we are going to make all this work. But what I'm saying is, will you give me another chance?'

Grabbing Daisy in a bear hug, Tom joined in her laughter.

'Daisy, I've waited so long to find someone like you.'

Bending towards her, Tom began gently kissing her neck, moving round to her lips. Leaning into him, Daisy felt her pulse race. The sense of being overwhelmed flooded her. Part of her seemed to lift itself from within and float away. Perhaps she was saying goodbye to her inner child? Or maybe it was Alex who had left, making way for Daisy to emerge. Whatever it was, she was captive to the arms holding her, yet never had she known such joy and freedom.

CHAPTER THIRTY ONE

'Tom tells me that you are a writer, Daisy, and you've been finishing a novel here.' Genevieve Weaver spoke in a soft, polished voice.

Tom's mother was an older version of Tabby and she could see where her daughter got her stunning looks. Nevertheless, her soft manner didn't still the apprehension Daisy was experiencing.

'Yes, I needed peace and quiet and Dad suggested Barley Ford. It's provided the background to finally complete it. Not to mention meeting such wonderful people, I'm not sure I have ever come across a place quite like it.'

Daisy sipped the velvety mulled wine, wishing she didn't feel like she was part of an inquisition.

'I hope the roguish wine isn't too strong? Spring in these parts can still be quite chilled. Nothing better for warming up a crowd of people who know little of each other. A trick I learned some years ago.'

Daisy steadily sipped at her drink. Curiosity mixed with a growing admiration for Tom's mother. She was nothing like she had expected, imagining her to be more lady of the manor than a homely farmer's wife. Then Daisy recalled that in truth, Tom's father was not really a farmer, but some hotshot banker or financier. No doubt Genevieve had spent many years perfecting her hostess skills. Curious though, thought Daisy, that she appeared so relaxed and affable. You could bump into her in the street and never think she had come from all this.

'I'm pleased Barley Ford has afforded you the respite you needed. Indeed, for generations, families have sought refuge here. I do miss the village,' Genevieve lamented.

'I can understand anyone missing being here. It borders on magical. I have thoroughly enjoyed being here.' Daisy risked a look across the room to where she could see Tom chatting animatedly with her dad.

'You'll be on your way soon then, I take it?'

'I am going to have to decide soon about heading home. I really need a holiday, but I haven't made any decisions yet. Still a few loose ends to sort out.'

Genevieve nodded, her eyes sliding across the room to Tom.

'Loose ends can often be left to float in the wind until it's time to tie them up. Don't be in too much of hurry, no one would blame you for lingering a little longer. Now if you'll excuse me, I need to rev Mrs B up to serve lunch.'

Daisy watched as her hostess confidently sashayed from the room, politely smiling at the guests as she did so. Her husband took a moment to whisper something in her ear, their eyes locked and her skin reddened slightly. Daisy felt like a voyeur glimpsing something private and intimate. She sighed quietly. To love someone so deeply, for so many years. It must be wonderful. Her insides were quivering. Did Tom's mother know about them? Was she giving them her blessing? Oh, it was all so confusing.

Glancing around the room, Daisy took a minute to observe the assembled throng. Dorothy was seated by the window, holding court. Harry firmly curled up on her knee. Gerald was standing by her side like a sentinel. Greg and Sarah were at the other end of the room, giggling and whispering. Nearer to the fireplace, her mother was laughing at something Ed had said. Even Joseph, Tom's father, appeared mesmerised by Olivia's presence. Astonishing to think this was her mother. Surprisingly, Daisy softened towards her and felt a glow of pride. If she had met this woman anywhere else and learned about her job, she would have been full of respect. She noticed her dad has his hand on her shoulder. Daisy inwardly smiled at her father's blatant declaration that she was his.

She wondered why he felt the need to do that. As mystifying

as her mother's life was, Daisy reluctantly gave way to the idea of what had been sacrificed. There still remained many questions, one being how she could be so calm after the anger that had raged inside for her so long? Ed had been proven right when he told her that she needed to hear her mother's version of events.

Tom sidled up beside her, sliding his hand around her waist and dropping a kiss on her cheek. She snuggled into him.

'So, what do you think of my mother?' he asked. 'She's impressive, don't you think?'

'Impressive, scary and yet she is very friendly. Does she know about us?'

'She worked it out. I guess you have featured in many of my conversations with her. The reason for the lunch was so she could suss you out.'

Startled by this comment, Daisy's eyes flashed wide open. She stared up at Tom, only to see him grinning.

'Sometimes, Daisy Tremaine, you are so easy to wind up. Come on, I reckon lunch is served.'

Following a long and convivial lunch, Daisy excused herself and headed outdoors towards the neglected kitchen garden.

Strolling around the paths, she was saddened by the neglect. Once it would have been a thriving and productive area. Although she was no gardener, there appeared to be a lot of work needed to regenerate it. Bringing it back to a successful, fertile piece of land would be a labour of love.

'Tabby, in her wisdom, has decided to pick up the gauntlet and make this her pet project.'

Spinning round, Daisy came face-to-face with Genevieve. An unexpected apprehension flooded through her. What if Tom hadn't been joking and she really was inspecting her?

'Tom told me this was your pride and joy at one time. It must be upsetting to see it like this.'

Genevieve threaded her arm through Daisy's and gently propelled her forward.

'It was. I spent every waking hour out here. Life was quite staid when Joseph was away. It kept me busy and healthy. Barley Ford is a wonderful place, but it has its limitations.'

Swallowing hard, Daisy muttered a banal reply.

'Let's sit down. I would love to hear your story Daisy.'

Judging it to be more of a command, Daisy followed Genevieve to a bench by a creeping honeysuckle. Taking in a gulp of air, she wondered how much she needed to share.

'It's complex, as stories go. I write, I'm successful. My mother left when I was ten. However, there is always a twist in the tale, and recently I found out that she had a secret life and has come back to make amends. Just general, run-of-the-mill family stuff.' A nervous laughed trilled from Daisy.

Genevieve crossed her legs and turned to face Daisy.

'It sounds like most families, to be truthful. Women have been making such dreadful decisions for centuries. Sacrifice is almost their watchword. We try to kid ourselves we are emancipated, but sometimes I wonder. Can you patch things up?'

Taken aback by her statement, Daisy noticed the older woman's eyes become glassy. Of course, she had given up much to support her own husband. Daisy hesitated before answering.

'It might need more than a patch. I was angry when she turned up unannounced and Dad has been less-than-honest with me all these years. Ed is the one who has helped me through this. Helping me to see more than just my own view point. One thing that I have learned is you cannot rage forever. It's early days, and truthfully, if I don't forgive, the danger is I will become bitter. I don't want to be that person. My dad doesn't deserve that. He brought me up and was always there, but it's difficult, as they have both conspired in the deceit. I wish my dad had been more up front in the early days. I need time to work it all out. I was watching my mum earlier, in the drawing room. It's hard to marry the woman who left to the one she presents today.'

'If it is any consolation, Daisy, I do understand some of your pain. And I can tell you that your mother is a remarkable woman.'

'Frankly, if my dad hadn't cared so much about her, loved her all this time, I may be saying something else. He could have become bitter and resentful, but he didn't. He stood by her. That says a lot, I guess.'

Genevieve reached out and took hold of Daisy's hand.

'I am sure this will come as no surprise to you, but I have known Olivia a long time. I met her when she first came here. Her heart was broken. She never heeded the advice given to her in the early days and one can assume her chickens have come home to roost. I confess, she appears less confrontational and more at peace with herself. Though I imagine coming here has stirred some painful memories.'

Daisy was only half surprised to hear this. It was becoming evident that most of the village knew of Olivia. One thing in her mother's favour was that no one spoke ill of her.

'She told me this is where she sought her sanctuary, to lick her wounds after the maelstrom of leaving Dad.'

Genevieve sighed, dropping Daisy's hand. Smoothing her dress, she stared out over the garden.

'I learned very early on when I married Joseph that I could flow with him or against him. I made my choice and we flowed around each other. None of it was easy. Our relationship ebbed and flowed. Almost tidal, you could say. I recognised something of myself in your mother when we eventually formed a friendship. She was lost. I remember her telling me how her whole life had fallen apart and there was no one to help her put it back together. We supported one another. However, she made the ultimate sacrifice and I am afraid I was more of a coward. I couldn't leave my children. I've never known how she did that.'

Daisy had a pounding in her chest. A great sense of sorrow swept through her.

'My dad didn't give her a choice. He basically told her to go and allowed no chance to make amends.'

Genevieve pulled a handkerchief from her pocket and dabbed her eyes.

'I'm pleased she found you, Genevieve. Irrespective of the outcome, we all need someone.'

A powerful feeling swelled up within Daisy and she rested her hand on Genevieve's shoulder.

'You'll work it out. I can see you are a bright girl. You have her steel running through you. Oh, and as if on cue, here comes someone to steal you away.'

Daisy turned to see Tom striding towards her. Her heart skipped a beat.

'Trust yourself with whatever decisions you have to make. Make them for you. They have to be the bedfellows we live with. I hope we shall see more of you, Daisy. Don't be a stranger.'

Standing up and walking away, Daisy noticed Genevieve gently squeeze Tom's arm as they passed each other.

'Had the guided tour then?' Tom fidgeted as he spoke.

'Yes. She's quite a lady your mum. Not as terrifying as I thought. Guess what? She knows my mum.'

Tom's deep echoing laugh reverberated around the garden.

'Well, I didn't know that. As for my mum, she is a pussy cat, believe me. Now if you want scary, just upset my dad.'

'She found me wandering out here. It's a sleeping space waiting to be awakened. Your mum tells me Tabby is taking it on. A bit the opposite of what I expected.'

'Yes, it is a contradiction, but Tabby is remarkably resourceful and determined. Can I walk you home? The others look set to be here all afternoon.'

Daisy smiled, and took his hand. Whilst her hand disappeared into his, the earthiness of him gave her a great sense of connection.

'I'd love that.'

CHAPTER THIRTY TWO

By the following mid-morning, Daisy was awash with new energy. It was as if the spring winds had blown the clouds far into the distance and presented her with a new landscape.

Having slept in the shadows as Daisy, the brightness of reconnecting with her former self was engaging and exciting. She knew that Tom was partly responsible for accessing the new sensations flooding her body. Just thinking of him made her heart race and forced her to beam the biggest smile. Nothing was certain, she knew that, but the day he walked into her life seemed to mark a change in how she viewed the world. Not to mention the patience Ed had demonstrated in listening and assisting her in opening her eyes.

Happy that Greg was still willing to press the pause button on things until she had spoken to her parents, Daisy began to sense a new momentum. When he and Sarah arrived home later in the evening, Daisy could see she was not the only one experiencing new desires.

Goosebumps travelled along her skin as she listened to a voicemail from Tom.

'How about a picnic later? Meet me at Jess's place by the river about one o'clock.'

Checking her watch, it was nearly ten. Knowing her parents would be here soon, she tidied things up. Taking a moment to look out of the kitchen window, she saw a flash of white streak by the fence. Tabby was at last giving Bentley the gallop he deserved.

Tom had explained to her before they parted company that Tabby would be sticking around for the foreseeable future. She knew it was time to take up the reins of assisting to run the estate.

'Financially, we just about keep our heads above water. What is required is investment, in the tenancies and the future. Tabby has at last accepted she bears the responsibility too. That's why she darted back to Scotland. Dad more or less called her out and told her in very harsh terms to consider her future.'

'He does sound very Victorian,' Daisy had suggested.

'No, he just believes that we are guardians of the land and its people and the tenant farmers rely upon us to be good managers. Good business sense really. Anyway, Tabby folded and so a new chapter in the Weaver family begins. I'm delighted to have her on board properly at last.'

The explanation about what Tabby actually did still remained hazy, something to do with translating and her uncanny ability to learn new languages speedily. As for Tom's dad, after speaking to his mum, it was obvious he was no banker. There was a link, she was sure, with her mum and even Tabby. Stories for another time. There was so much of her own still to write.

Life-changing decisions were popping up all over the place. Tom had created a business plan around building the holiday rental business, while Tabby had managed to talk her father into plans to develop another disused barn. Her idea to refurb and offer it as a family unit had met a nod of approval from the rest of the family. It had been her leverage for staying. Added to that, she wanted to offer riding holidays and trekking for disabled children. There had been relief in his voice as he had explained the plans.

Daisy had reached a conclusion that the price for her growing fame was to always be on her guard, protecting those around her. Although some of the pressure had been distilled by asking Greg to hold off on announcements, Daisy knew there were huge changes ahead. A revelation had hit her late in the night as she had tossed and turned. Although she was still puzzled by the reaction between her mum and Ed, it was as if she could suddenly see what it must have been like for her mum leading a dual existence. A clearer picture was beginning to emerge of what her mother had experienced all those years ago. Accepting that her mum was back had also surprised Daisy. Deep down inside her, a younger Daisy was dancing in the street at the prospect of having her mum around.

A knock on the front door caused her nerves to jangle.

'Hi there, Daisy button.'

Her dad strode in, followed by her mum.

Hugging each other in the hallway, Daisy was aware of being more relaxed.

'Have you got that kettle on?'

Daisy groaned; she had never known anyone drink so much tea.

'You and Tom disappeared pretty sharpish after lunch yesterday,' her mother enquired.

'Yes, we had a lot of talking to do. Or rather, I had some explaining to do. You didn't mention you knew his mum.'

Olivia shrugged a shoulder, 'Didn't I?'

'What's happening then Daisy?' asked Dan, perching on a bar stool.

'The book is done. Well, it was, until I had this epiphany and decided to change the ending. Caused Greg a bit of hysteria, but we've worked things out.'

'Well done, that's my girl. I knew you would get there in the end. Barley Ford was a good idea then?' Dan said, grinning.

'Yes, it was in so many ways.' Daisy mirrored her father's grinning face.

'I have been a crazy, demented harridan at times and I am genuinely sorry. The best thing you could ever have done was recommend this place. Retreating here, licking my wounds, it allowed me to grasp that life is not always straightforward. I'm not saying it will all be plain sailing from now on, but at least we all have a starting point. I genuinely hope we can build our bridges. Discussing my issues with Ed has been hugely beneficial. Who would have thought chatting to a stranger would have such an impact on an individual? So much of what has gone into the Chronicles mirrored my own story. When I met Tom, it was like a light going on in the darkness. He is everything I could have ever wished for. During our conversations it became clear to me how much this place means to him, he is part of something. It's not in isolation, it's a panoramic view of the future. That's when I realised how minute my world is, I have never lived my own life and done anything.'

Pausing to steady herself, Daisy carried on.

'I'm taking a break and travelling. Just me, no one else. I've inhabited so much of the world from the stories you've shared Dad, your adventures in foreign parts. I need to seek out my own vistas and stories. As Daisy Tremaine, not Alex Dennison.'

A hush settled on the room. Daisy had been worried the anxiety might creep in, but so far it was keeping its distance.

'I'm not sure I was expecting that but I think it's a great idea. Well done you. Your mum and I are very proud.' Dan stood up and went to give Daisy a hug.

'Oh, Daisy darling, I've only just got here and it seems you are the one leaving this time. But I get what you need to do. Are you really going alone?'

'Yes, I am. I'm meeting Tom at lunch to tell him my plans. I hope he understands.'

Olivia slid off the kitchen stool and walked over to Daisy. Taking her hands in her own, she drew her daughter close to her.

'If he loves you my sweet girl, he will understand. Love is a strange companion at times, but those who truly love us let us go when they need to. I don't think he is going anywhere.'

Daisy held her mother's gaze. Then something clicked in her head. She was speaking about Ed. With a gentle nod of her head, Daisy acknowledged to her mum that she understood.

Dan opened his case and pulled out a bottle of champagne.

'I've been saving this for a very special occasion. Grab the glasses Daisy and let's toast the future.'

CHAPTER THIRTY THREE

Daisy could barely contain herself as she raced along the path to meet Tom. It was hard to comprehend what was happening to her. In her wildest moments she had never expected her life to flip and change the way it had.

Her parents were on their way back to Lytton, content in the knowledge Daisy was recovering from her anxiety and finding her feet. It was their turn now to work out their lives. How things would evolve between them was in the air. Daisy had an inkling about the relationship between her mother and Ed. When her mum was ready to tell her what had happened between them, she would be ready to listen.

Arriving at last to the little oasis she had discovered by chance, she spread out the blanket she had brought with her. Sitting down with her legs stretched out before her, Daisy tilted her head. The weak sunlight washed over her, soothing and comforting her. She wanted to bank the sensation and hold it forever.

As if she had wished him here, she heard Jess bark before being jumped on and lathered in doggy licks. Falling back, she burst out laughing.

'Jess, Jess, okay girl, I'm pleased to see you too.'

A whistle heralded the arrival of Tom. Straightaway, Jess flicked her head towards her master and jumped off Daisy.

'That dog has great taste.' Smirking, Tom lowered himself by Daisy and placed his rucksack down by his side.

Opening it, he produced a small dish for Jess, who eagerly tucked into her surprise treat.

Unscrewing the lid from a flask, he poured Daisy a cup of hot soup.

'Mrs B insisted it was not the weather for picnics, so handed me her leek and potato soup, freshly made this morning. She has even baked a crusty loaf.'

'Thank you to Mrs B.' Daisy blew across the top of the cup.

'So here we are. Thanks for agreeing to this,' Tom said quietly.

Jess sprawled out beside Tom and Daisy was oddly moved by her devotion.

'It was a great idea. Have your parents gone?' Changing her position, Daisy sat crossed-legged, facing Tom.

'No. Dad is not one to let the grass grow on an idea, he's busy drawing up plans for the conversion and Tabby is arranging to meet an architect. All systems go.' Tom gazed across the river.

'You sound doubtful.' Daisy asked quietly.

'Only regarding Tabby, she's not used to staying anywhere for too long. I just hope she means what she says this time. We've been here before. After a few weeks, she gets itchy feet and whoosh, she's off. Mrs B has filled the red tin and another one besides. She fears Tabby may have a few outbursts.'

'Mrs B knows her very well. Perhaps Tabby at last realises what home means. If you had seen her with Dorothy, you would think it was another person.'

Sipping her soup, Daisy ruminated on Tom's words, she was even more convinced she had reached a workable compromise regarding her future plans.

'You ready to share what you are up to, Daisy? The women in my life seem determined to torture me.' Grinning, he pulled off a chunk of bread and began munching.

'I'm not going to pretend everything has miraculously sorted itself out. I have a plan and once it was clear in my head, I realised Sarah was right, it is this simple. Then I explained it to Greg. But what has to be accepted is that my decisions have consequences for others.'

'How so? You can write anywhere. You've proved that by living in Barley Ford.'

'Yes, that part can be done wherever my mojo works. It's the rest. All the add-on bits that go with being a successful writer. Barley Ford is not the most accessible place. Catching a train is not exactly easy. Then there is my time out.'

'The train station is half an hour away. Okay, you have to

change trains, but it is doable. As for time out... what does that mean?'

Daisy searched Tom's face for anything that would make this easier. All she could see was hope shining from his eyes. Oh, those deep, dreamy treacle eyes. Losing herself in those was a paradise waiting to be unearthed.

As if reading her thoughts, Tom leant forward and kissed her tenderly on her lips. Inside, the sweet melting ache of desire stirred with alarming speed. It took a great deal of self-control to keep on track with what she wanted to say.

'I have decided to take a time out and with Greg's agreement, he is going to pause all the madness building around the movie discussions and the proposed book launch. There are some edits to be done, the cover to sort, but basically, he's agreed it can work.'

'What exactly does a time out mean Daisy?' Tom shifted his own position.

Watching him like a cat, Daisy's familiar knot of tension began to wind itself inside her chest.

'I'm going alone Tom. I need to do this alone. I need to explore the world as Daisy. Not Alex. She has overshadowed me for far too long. I've relied too much on her. It was something Ed said to me. I've been cosseted, afraid of my own shadow. I didn't want to be me because everyone ran away from me. I can see how that was a dramatic response. But it's time for me to give her a break. Daisy is breaking out.' Daisy tried to laugh, but Tom was frowning.

'You are still not answering my question about us.'

Leaning into Tom, Daisy encircled him with her arms and tugged him back onto the blanket.

'Oh, I think this will answer everything,' she whispered, smothering his face in kisses.

In the early evening, Daisy was busy packing her case upstairs when she heard a knock at the door.

Opening it, she was surprised to see Dorothy and Harry.

'Dorothy what a lovely surprise. Please come in. Let's sit in the front lounge.'

'Thank you my dear. I wanted to catch you before you go. It is tomorrow you are leaving?'

'Sadly. It's strange, now it has come to it, I don't want to go.'

Dorothy sat herself down in the armchair by the fire.

'Have you lit this fire every evening?'

'Yes, it is so comforting. How are you doing? No stick, is that wise?'

'Probably not. Anyway, Harry has proven himself to be quite the guardian. Truth be Daisy, I wanted to check how you are? I appreciate it has been a confusing time for you. So much uncertainty, the deceit. Oh yes, your mother filled me in. I had an idea it was Olivia who was your mother. I knew her from her time here. It made Gerald's day when she popped up.'

Daisy dropped onto the window seat as she was drawing the curtains. A familiar tugging sensation skated around her.

'You know Dorothy, I am not in the least surprised, though I'm concerned about what you may have to say. It appears most people here know her. Everyone seems to know stuff except me. It's been like wandering through Wonderland.'

'You and your mother will work things out. One thing I can tell you about her is that she is very determined. And she's fearless too. You want her on your side, I can tell you that. When she does eventually share her adventures, I think you will be quite astounded. What about you though? I hear you are taking a long holiday.'

Daisy laughed. 'Barley Ford network at it again. Have you been talking to Tom?'

'No, as a matter of fact, his mother. Genevieve is very good at rooting out what is going on. She should have been the one working for the firm, not Joseph. I hear she is staying for a while. They seemed to have finally tamed the wild Tabitha.'

Daisy instantly sat up.

'Again, I'm not shocked. I had my suspicions. Tom never said anything.'

Daisy's heartrate increased, immediately thinking Tom had not trusted her enough to tell her.

Before you start thinking the worst of Tom, I'm telling you because I think, given the circumstances, you should know. Joseph worked for the diplomatic service. Nothing like the world Olivia was in, however, there were times he moved in circles which brought him in collision with Olivia. Tabby is an interpreter and has worked for the firm since she left university. She was recruited in her final year. Tom has no idea about the firm, it's better that way.'

Daisy rubbed her hands together to try and control their trembling. Just when you think you have everything worked out, along comes a curve you never saw.

'Why is it better? And more to the point, why do you think I should know?'

'Joseph and Genevieve have spent their whole lives living in an intricate web of misdirections. I know how fond Tom is of you. I can see the love budding and just observing you both, it's clear you are made for each other. I told you at the beginning of your stay here that forgiveness is a wonderful thing if you can be brave enough to do it. For your life to work in conjunction with Tom and his family, you will need trust, forgiveness and patience. For you to consider Barley Ford as your home, you will need equal amounts of all three. Above all else, you need to forgive yourself, Daisy, and live your life.'

Daisy sat very still watching the flames dance up the back of the chimney. When she set out to find herself, it had been to allow her the time to complete the book – and to consider the possibility of never writing another word. In the new beginning, she had found so much more. She realised she had found her family again. Yet Dorothy felt like family too.

'Daisy, you are like the daughter I never had. I have grown very fond of you. This cottage will always be here for you. It belongs to Gerald. He spent many happy hours here in the old days. He couldn't bear for it to be sold off to a stranger, so he bought it. We have discussed it and both agree it is the perfect bolthole for you for the time being, until things become more permanent. When you leave tomorrow, a part of you will remain here and you will collect it when you return.'

Without warning, Harry scrambled up onto Daisy's knee. Catching her unawares, a tear trickled down her cheek. She would come back. This place and the people in it had wedged themselves in her heart. Apart from which, there were more stories to uncover. She had enough material to fire her imagination for years to come. More importantly though, she had made deep, long-lasting relationships and that was more valuable than anything.

CHAPTER THIRTY FOUR

Languishing on the sun lounger, Daisy lifted her hat from over her eyes to watch the waves lap the white sand. Daring to step out of the shadows and back into her life as Daisy hadn't been an easy path. She had left Daisy, still aged eighteen, on a roadside somewhere. Meeting up with her again now, approaching her thirties, was an immense transition.

The best thing she could ever have done was admit her need to talk to someone about the pain which riveted her to the past. She had been really scared when Sarah suggested she needed to speak to someone. Daisy never imagined she needed therapy, thinking it was for people who had much more serious issues than her own. Yet her own problems were major. She understood she had never come to terms with her mum walking out and leaving no explanation. It was plain abandonment, no matter her reasons for doing it.

Sliding an envelope from between the pages of the book she was reading, she unfolded the letter and read it once more.

It had been a shock to receive it.

Dear Daisy,
Ordinarily, I wouldn't write to a client. On this occasion however, I decided it was prudent. Dorothy tells me she has explained a few things about Tom's family. It appears you have been entrusted with a secret that was not Dorothy's to share, although I know she had your best interest at heart.
I took it upon myself to speak with Genevieve, as asking you to withhold such secrets is no way for you to begin your relationship with Tom, especially given everything you have been through in this way. She has agreed that Joseph will speak to Tom, after which I hope he will explain it to you. I would suggest you feign ignorance.

Barley Ford is no ordinary village, you understand that now. In being drawn into its web you will be required to keep many things close to your heart and that can sometimes be enough to break people. Remember when you asked me if hearts could burst with pain? I'm glad you heart is starting to heal, but that doesn't mean you're not prone to a crack or two.
Enjoy your well-earned rest and we'll talk when you return.
Best wishes, Ed.

Staring out to sea, Daisy was trying to remain steadfast in her belief that she would be able to cope. Slipping the letter back in its envelope, she wedged it in her bag.

Making the decision to walk away so soon after reconciling with her mum had been difficult. It was still a bumpy road for the two of them, and occasionally Daisy was still reminded of all the lonely nights she and her dad had spent missing her. The missed birthdays, Christmases, and yet the whole time her dad had known her mother was somewhere watching from a distance.

It had been a complete surprise to learn about Blueberry Cottage. She was over the moon, as she had become quite attached to its comforting ambience. Knowing she had a bolthole there, which Dorothy was keeping an eye on, made her feel safe. Fortunately, life was carrying on with no repercussions from Daisy's time living there. Greg had been as good as his word, playing it all very low-key. He was assisted by Sarah, who kept the website and blog of Alex ticking over perfectly. She had voiced her concerns to them both that someone would find out where she was and the serenity of Barley Ford would be blown apart. But they assured her that Barley Ford would be protected from any intrusions.

Daisy chuckled to herself, thinking that Greg and Sarah made an awesome team. She had a hunch they might be engaged quite soon.

She was relieved that Tom and Tabby had undertaken an impressive programme of works on the farm. Tabby had agreed to shadow him and eventually look to sharing things more broadly. She was also pleased that, for now, Tom's doubts were allayed.

Travelling for the last three months had brought Daisy to the final leg of her journey. She had taken a train through Europe. It was excessive and indulgent, but it had been a great way to travel. Venice had captured her heart; Florence, Rome and Paris had satiated her thirst for art and history.

Flying out to the Maldives was madness on her part, but luxuriating in its glamour and beauty had made it worth her while.

As Tom dropped down next to her, she turned to face him. The water glistened on his skin.

'You looked miles away.' He gently removed her hat and leaned in to peck her cheek.

'I was being reflective.'

'Well, how about reflecting on this?'

Rolling on top of Daisy, Tom began smothering her in hungry kisses. She was suddenly glad they had a secluded cove.

Responding to Tom's ardent passion, Daisy packed away her apprehension about the life she had yet to face, along with ideas for the next book, which were burning their way through her brain.

Stopping suddenly, Tom scooped Daisy up into his arms and carried her back to the small bungalow perched at the edge of the sand.

Could life be any dreamier than this? she thought.

Kicking the door shut, he laid Daisy on the bed. A long, low sigh emitted from her. He only had a few days to spend with her and it had been a feat of logistics to get him here, but he had agreed. When she had first explained to Tom that she had meant it when she said she wanted to travel alone, he had been devastated. However, once she had explained that she hoped he would join her at some point on her journey, he had been ecstatic.

'Don't go anywhere, I'll be back.'

Blissfully happy, Daisy allowed herself a certain amount of satisfaction.

'I decided we needed strawberries.' Tom grinned, standing in the doorway. His taut, muscular body caused wild sensations to spark throughout her body.

'Tom Weaver, who would have thought it?'

For the moment, as Tom rained his kisses all over her, interrupted only by the strawberry juice, it was just her story with Tom. She didn't know where life would take them, but for now, he was prince enough for Daisy Tremaine.

EPILOGUE

Olivia leant against the ancient stones of the old pack bridge and dropped a rose into the slow flow of the river.

'Sill think the river carries hearts to heaven, Liv?'

Contemplating her answer, Olivia slowly turned to her companion. Placing her gloved hand to his cheek, she stared into his grey-flecked eyes.

'It carried me here. And isn't this a little piece of heaven?'

Ed tenderly took her hand and removed the glove. Kissing the back of her hand, he raised his eyes and watched as Olivia sank a little against the bridge.

'Please don't, this is hard enough as it is.'

Dropping her hand, Ed leant into Olivia and brought her into his arms.

'You shouldn't have come back Olivia. I warned you what would happen if you did. Do you think Daisy has worked things out?'

Ed felt her body stiffen.

'Not everything. She'll be back herself next week.

'You know, just because we become adults Ed, it doesn't mean we get it right, does it?'

'No, it doesn't. It's all about damage limitation.'

Olivia rested her head on Ed's shoulder.

'I have to go.' She took hold of his arms and gently pulled them away.

'Technically, you don't. You know that.'

Olivia nodded. Kissing him on the cheek, she turned to walk away.

'I still love you.' His voice was husky as he clung onto her hand.

'I know Ed, I love you too. Would that it was that simple.'

'It is that simple Olivia, we just make it hard on ourselves.'

'I don't know how to do simple, Ed.' Tears trickled down her cheeks.

'Then I shall have to teach you when you come back.' Ed used his thumb to banish the tears.

'I may not come back.'

'You will, you have every reason to now.'

Walking away, Olivia sensed a shift in her universe. So much deception. Her life had been built on it. She had no idea about her future, except that it now included Daisy and that made her feel even more nervous. When everything was finally in the open, she knew she would have nowhere to run.

ACKNOWLEDGEMENTS

This story has evolved over many, many months. It has been cajoled and nurtured with the help of friends who have read my drafts.

The Beverley Chapter of the RNA. A great bunch of writers who welcomed me.

Alison May, who was honest and constructive.

The friends who were my beta readers and read with honesty.

Mandy Appleyard, for taking the time to show and not tell.

To Catherine and Katharine and Rachel for at last bringing this story to life.

Coming soon,
in 2022…

Edward's Story,
Book Two of the
Barley Ford series.

www.ingramcontent.com/pod-product-compliance
Lightning Source LLC
Chambersburg PA
CBHW021436080526
44588CB00009B/541